IGNITE

Refining and Purifying Your Faith

**A SMALL-GROUP STUDY
BY ED YOUNG**

Ignite: Refining and Purifying Your Faith
© 2005 Edwin B. Young

Published by Serendipity House Publishers
Nashville, Tennessee

In cooperation with Fellowship Church Resources
Dallas, Texas

ISBN: 1-5749-4191-7

Dewey Decimal Classification: 248.84
Subject Headings:
CHRISTIAN LIFE \ FAITH \ PROVIDENCE AND GOVERNMENT OF GOD

1-800-525-9563
www.SerendipityHouse.com

www.fellowshipchurch.com

Printed in the United States of America
11 10 09 08 07 06 05   1 2 3 4 5 6 7 8 9 10

CONTENTS

HOW TO USE THIS BOOK

Small groups are a vital part of how we do ministry at Fellowship Church just as they are in many churches around the world. There are a number of different theories on how small groups should work, and they are all great in different ways. The book you are holding is written with our model in mind. So take a minute to read the following explanation, then feel free to adapt as necessary.

Each of our small groups practices a three-part agenda in every meeting. That agenda includes a social time, a discussion time, and a prayer time. Each of these elements share equal importance, but not necessarily equal time. To help you get the most out of this book, we have included an explanation of each of the parts.

The first element of every small-group meeting should be a time of socializing. This phase of the meeting should be about 30% of your time together. Welcome everyone as they arrive at the host home; make visitors feel welcome by introducing yourself and showing genuine interest in them. Enjoy some snacks, or if your group prefers, a meal together. Then move on to the second part of the meeting—the lesson.

The lesson itself may take as much as 50% of your group's meeting time. You may want to start this phase with a short "icebreaker" to get everyone talking. The questions in the "Start It Up" section of each session are what we refer to as "level the playing field" questions that everyone can participate in, regardless of their level of spiritual maturity or Bible knowledge. As your group moves through the "Talk It Up" section in each meeting, remember that it is more important to finish on time than to finish each question. It is okay to skip some questions to allow enough time to take care of the third phase of your small-group time: "Lift It Up."

The "Lift It Up" section is a vital part of every small-group meeting and should take about 20% of your time. You will be able to share with the group what God is doing in your life as well as asking the group to support you in specific prayers. To help focus this time, there are one or two questions that will prompt prayers based on the material you just covered. There is also a space for you to write down your prayer requests so you don't forget them and so you can communicate them clearly when it is your turn. Below that is a place to write down the prayer requests of the people in your group so you can remember to pray for each request throughout the week.

As an additional tool to assist you in your spiritual development journey, 10 devotionals lead up to each of the Sessions 2 through 8. Ten devotionals are provided to accommodate groups that meet every other week, giving material for five days per week during that two-week interval. If you meet weekly, ask your group members to choose at least five devotionals each week. These will help you develop a daily quiet time with God. To get the absolute most from this book, I challenge you to take 5 or 10 minutes a day to read and apply these devotionals in your life.

God's best!
Ed

IGN|TE

Refining and Purifying Your Faith

I stood there motionless, my legs completely frozen. A mere three feet in front of me was a man who could have easily crushed me with one hand. This guy had fists the size of my head, a neck the size of my waist, and biceps the size of my thighs. And he was throwing punches in rapid-fire succession directly at my face—coming so close I could feel the wind rushing past my ears!

No, I wasn't in a street fight. I was standing in front of a professional boxer who was warming up for his next bout. His manager was a friend of mine, and he had invited me into the locker room so that I could experience a little of what it's like to go toe-to-toe with a heavyweight fighter. Talk about an adrenaline rush!

When it comes to life, most of us want to experience it, don't we? We're not content with just sitting on the sidelines. We want to be in the game. Even the world of advertising capitalizes on this desire to experience life—they push us to drive the car that will let us feel the road or strap on the shoes that will help us feel like we're walking on air.

When it comes to faith, God wants you to experience the ultimate rush—the daily rush of living completely and passionately for Christ. He doesn't want you to sit on the sidelines as the world flies by. He wants to spark a burning desire and ignite a white-hot fire in your heart. That's exactly what this study is all about.

You are going to discover just how to catch a spiritual spark from lives of some unique characters in Scripture, and then fan those flames of faith until they burn white hot for Christ. You're going to learn how to get off the sidelines, get into the game, and experience the passion of a life totally devoted to Him.

5

IGNITE

Refining and Purifying Your Faith

What Floats Your Boat? ... Listening to God (Noah)

Genesis 6:5-7:5; 8:13-22

At one time or another, most of us experience "dry spells"—times when our lives feel flat and meaningless. Maybe you're a new Christ-follower. You've taken the first step on your journey of faith and you are wondering what on earth to do next. Or, maybe you've been a Christ-follower for quite a while. You believe in Jesus and bowed to His rule in your life a long time ago. Yet now you are feeling a little bit "burned out." Maybe you've been going through some tough times, or you've been too busy to think much about God. You just don't have the fire and enthusiasm you felt at the beginning.

Sometimes we forget that being a Christ-follower means just that: following. We take the first step and then we just sit there—wondering why we don't have passion and victory in our spiritual lives. Over the next several weeks, we will look at the lives of some "faith giants" in the Bible. From their lives we can find both encouragement and practical help for becoming "fired up" men and women of God.

START IT UP

Most of us have probably gotten into an argument with someone about "hearing" versus "listening." "You're not listening to me!" ... "I heard what you said the first time!" ... "Why don't you ever listen to me?"

1. Have you ever had a dog or other pet? Did this pet come when you called or did it totally ignore you? Would it come for anybody else?

2. **When you are in a crowded room, is there one particular sound you are more likely to notice than other sounds? Why?**

TALK IT UP

Noah was a man that God used to do great things. We can look at Noah's life and see one outstanding characteristic: Noah could hear God's voice. He knew how to listen to God. God wants to do great things in each of our lives. This is a transforming truth that we each need to own and apply. But if God is going to do great things through us, we'd better learn how to hear His voice clearly. Noah's life illustrates four benefits of listening to God.

Read Genesis 6:5-7:5; 8:13-22

Benefit 1: A God's Eye View

The first benefit of listening to God is that it **provides us with perspective.**

When we make something and we don't like the way it turns out, we often react destructively. We get frustrated with our projects and we trash them. Genesis 6:6 says, "the Lord was grieved that He had made man on the earth." We might think that God's first reaction would be like ours: frustration and then extermination. God is a God of justice—He could not allow wickedness to go on and on without dealing with it. But He is also a God of mercy, grace, and forgiveness. He decided to wipe out the people He had put on earth, but He also chose to save those who were following Him.

Genesis 6:8 says "But Noah found favor in the eyes of the LORD." Noah was chosen for an incredible assignment because he walked with God and knew God personally. Like Noah, we desperately need to have God's perspective in every slice of our lives—from our relationships, to what is going on in our businesses, to what is going on in our thought lives.

When Noah began to build the ark, his neighbors probably thought he was crazy. Here he was, 500 years old, starting to build a giant boat and claiming that God was going to destroy the world. He sounds like the classic crank and everyone was no doubt laughing at him. From a human perspective, being ridiculed was enough reason for Noah to quit building the ark. But Noah wasn't seeing from a human perspective; he was living from God's "big picture" perspective. To everyone else, he looked like a crazy old man building a boat that would never float. From God's perspective, Noah was an obedient servant, getting ready for the catastrophe that would certainly happen.

3. **Have you ever done something that other people thought was crazy? What was your perspective on the situation? What do you think God's perspective was?**

Benefit 2: Staying Power

Listening to God also **empowers us with endurance**. Have you ever thought about how long it actually took Noah to build his ark? 120 years! Most of us would get tired of the project after 12 years—or 12 months. We want to see results, we want proof that what we are doing really matters. Every great man or woman of God has sometimes struggled with doubt and thoughts of quitting. However, because Noah was listening to God's perspective, God gave him the endurance he needed. Endurance gives us the ability to crash through quitting points. Often life is like running a marathon. We get along fine for the first 20 miles, and then we hit the "wall" and think that if we have to keep running we are going to die. "There is no way I can persevere in this marriage situation, this job, this relationship. I just can't do this any more. I just want to lie down and die. I'm done." But the Holy Spirit will be right there encouraging us to keep running, to keep enduring, to break through the wall. So many times if we crash through that "brick" wall, we look back and see that it was made of paper.

4. **When have you pushed past a "quitting point"? How big does that wall or obstacle look to you now from this side?**

Noah stuck with it 120 long years—until the ark was done. He didn't spend those 120 years worrying about how he was going to get the animals into it. He didn't spend every Friday practicing his tiger catching skills or making a checklist of all the animals. He just built the boat and when the right time came, the Bible says that God brought the animals to Noah. God arranged everything; all Noah had to do was obey ... one step at a time. We too need to simply do what we know God wants us to do. Too often we say, "Well, I just don't know if I think this will really work. How am I going to deal with these things? What if such and such happens? I need to know what I should do." God's answer is really simple: "I'll take care of the overall plan. You start by doing what I said to do."

5. **When has God given you a "build the boat" assignment? How did you respond to the details?**

6. **What types of details do you worry or wonder about as you think about trying to obey God in your current circumstances?**

Benefit 3: Perfect Timing

Another benefit of listening to God is that listening **teaches us timing**. Most of us don't understand the difference between God's timing and ours. We want things now, on our timing. We want the perfect mate now. We want to advance in our careers now. We want to be healed and have all our problems solved right now. But God says, "Wait and walk with Me and at the right time I will do the right thing." God is never early and He is never late, He is always on time. Noah went into the ark when God said to—not before, not after. He waited for seven days before anything happened. Altogether, he lived in that boat for over a year. Many times he must have been impatient to get off and to look for some land, but he waited. He didn't move until God said, "It's time."

7. **When have you seen an example of the difference between God's timing and your timing? Was it worth the wait?**

Benefit 4: Loving Hearts

Listening to God **leads us to love**. Noah's first action after he landed on dry ground demonstrates his love for God. He knew salvation came from God and his response was to build an altar to honor and thank Him. Noah gave his best animals and sacrificed them. It's easy to pray when the seas are rocky or in a life and death situation. But, when all is well, we tend to put God in a closet and go our merry ways. Instead, the good times should be the times when we give God our best. We should be expressing our love in praise, thanksgiving, and obedience to God. People who listen to God are people who know God and those who know God want to praise Him with their lives.

8. **What do you think your first reaction would be if you were stepping on dry ground again after a year on a boat with a bunch of smelly animals?**

9. **How can you demonstrate an attitude of thankfulness and worship in your day-to-day life?**

Learning to Listen

We've discovered four benefits of listening to God—but how do we actually do it?

(1) First, we have to ***accept God's invitation***. The ark is a picture of salvation. God offered a gracious invitation and Noah accepted. In the same way, God has given us Jesus Christ as the "ark" to escape His wrath against sin. If we accept the invitation and step on board, we enter into relationship with Him. It is impossible to hear God's voice if you are not in relationship with Him.

(2) We also have to ***remove barriers in our lives***. Our sins create a barrier between God and us. If there is any sin in our lives that we have not dealt with, it will impede our hearing God. When we sin—and we will—we have to tear down the barrier by confessing our sins to God and repenting. To "repent" means turning around and going the other way. With a lifestyle of repentance, you commit to having no communication barriers between God and yourself.

(3) Finally, we must ***train our ears***. Studies show that newborn infants' ears are trained to pick out the voices of their mothers, fathers, and siblings. A mother's ears are trained to hear the unique sound of her baby's cries. A person may sleep through a thunderstorm, yet hear the faint click before the morning alarm snaps on. Your hear the sounds that matter most to you.

A story is told of a man from the country and a city man walking around the big city. The two men are walking down a street jammed with traffic when suddenly the man from the country stops. "Wait—I hear a cricket." His friend says, "What? No way, not in city." "Yes, I hear a cricket." Sure enough, at the base of a skyscraper, a blade of grass juts through a crack in the sidewalk and a little cricket is chirping his heart out. The city man is blown away. "How did you hear that?" And his friend said, "I'll show you how." He takes two pennies from his pocket, and drops them on the ground. When the money hits the sidewalk, heads jerk around, people stop, ears perk up. He picks up the money off the sidewalk and says, "You hear what your ear is trained to hear."

10. **Whose voices are your ears trained to hear?**

11. **As you honestly evaluate your life, what things grab your attention and ignite your passion?**

LIFT IT UP

So, are you ready to take the first big step toward igniting your passion and purifying your faith? Are you listening to God? Are you starting your days and your ways with the question, "What do You want, God?" or do you do your own thing and ask God to bless it? Let's take another step down the road of following Christ, and learn to really listen.

12. **What kind of training have you been giving your ears? How much time do you spend each day focused on your relationship with God?**

13. **Do you think you might have some communication barriers between you and God? Ask Him to show you the sins in your life and then confess them to Him and repent.**

Take time to pray together, asking God to help each of you learn to really listen to Him—to devote regular time and energy to strengthening your relationship with God, as well as to train your ears. Invite God to reveal barriers to listening and help you confess and turn back toward Him.

My Prayer Needs:

_____

_____

My Group's Prayer Needs:

_____

_____

_____

_____

_____

DEVOTIONALS

DAY 1: **Hydrating Your Soul**

O God, you are my God, earnestly I seek you; my soul thirsts for you, my body longs for you, in a dry and weary land where there is no water (Psalm 63:1).

Have you ever been thirsty—really, seriously thirsty? Even if we've never come close to the black, swollen tongue stage, we all know what it's like to thirst for a cool drink of water. Imagine yourself in a "dry and weary land where there is no water" and your throat will begin to feel dry.

The Bible is to our souls what water is to the body. It's essential for us to grow spiritually. Without constant communication with God, our souls dry up and we become weak and thirsty. Do you listen for God's voice with the same regularity that you drink water? Do you know how to keep your soul hydrated?

If you don't have a plan for spending time with God each day, now is a great time to start. Even a few minutes a day will help you keep on track. List some ideas to make this a daily part of your life.

_____

_____

_____

_____

_____

_____

_____

_____

_____

_____

_____

_____

_____

_____

_____

_____

_____

_____

DEVOTIONALS

DAY 2: **Who's Really in Charge?**

Why do you call me, "Lord, Lord," and do not do what I say? (Luke 6:46).

We all know the saying, "Actions speak louder than words." But we sometimes act as though God is blind or on vacation. We say the right words, but don't follow up with right actions. Don't fool yourself. God isn't far away. It's great to acknowledge God, but it doesn't mean much if you don't live out God's ways. If you mean it when you say, "Jesus is Lord," you are saying "Jesus is my boss. He has both the power and the authority to be my master." The word "Lord" simply means "master." You are acknowledging that He is in charge.

Ask God to reveal areas where you are not listening to and following Him. Where do you most need to adjust?

DEVOTIONALS

DAY 3: **Rock Solid**

I will show you what he is like who comes to me and hears my words and puts them into practice. He is like a man building a house, who dug down deep and laid the foundation on rock. When a flood came, the torrent struck the house but could not shake it, because it was well built (Luke 6:47-48).

Jesus knew that people like pictures, so He often painted word pictures to help us understand spiritual truths. If you know anything about building a house, you know that the foundation is the most crucial part of the structure. If the foundation is not level or square, walls will not be level or square. As each story is added, the errors become greater until the house twists, sags, and eventually falls.

Our lives are like houses. If we don't have an adequate foundation, we are going to crash when hard times come. Think of Jesus' words as the advice of a master builder. If we do what He says and dig our foundations deep, we build our worldview, morals, and actions on the solid rock of who He is. We'll be able to stand firm and stay calm when life threatens to overwhelm us.

Think of an area in your life where you need help standing firm and staying calm. Ask God to show you how to be obedient and to stand strong on His foundation.

_____

_____

_____

_____

_____

_____

_____

_____

_____

_____

_____

_____

DEVOTIONALS

DAY 4: **Swept Away**

But the one who hears my words and does not put them into practice is like a man who built a house on the ground without a foundation. The moment the torrent struck that house, it collapsed and its destruction was complete (Luke 6:49).

Human beings seem obsessed with security. We buy insurance for everything from fires to alien abductions. We try to plan our finances and our retirement so that we will always be "safe." We wear seat belts and helmets, buy special ultraviolet protection sun-cream, drink broccoli sprout juice to fight cancer, and lobby for the reduction of environmental hazards. We try to protect ourselves from life's storms, but that is impossible. We get cancer, lose someone we love, or see our homes burn down. Catastrophe can strike at any minute. The question is: how are you going to handle it? Do you trust your preparations to save you from disaster or do you have something more to hold onto when the waves beat against your house?

In who or what do you really trust? Whom do you really obey? What can you change to make sure that it is God you are depending on, and not your own precautions?

_____

_____

_____

_____

_____

_____

_____

_____

_____

_____

_____

_____

_____

_____

_____

_____

DEVOTIONALS

DAY 5: **I Know That Voice**

My sheep listen to my voice; I know them, and they follow me (John 10:27).

Jesus promised us that whoever turned their lives over to Him would be like His sheep. They would learn to recognize His voice and follow Him. Sometimes we struggle—wondering whether God is really talking to us. We don't hear audible voices. We don't receive e-mails from heaven providing step-by-step directions for life. We know God usually speaks to us in a more subtle manner. But how can we be sure it is really His voice?

How do you recognize your spouse's voice or your best friend's? You know that person's voice because you have communicated extensively with him or her. When you pick up the phone you know who it is just by the way he or she says "hello." It's the same with learning to know the voice of Jesus. The more time you spend talking and listening to Him, the easier it will become to recognize His voice. In fact, you probably already know His voice better than you think.

What things would Jesus never tell you to do? How do you know? What sorts of things might He be likely to say? Spend time just listening right now.

DEVOTIONALS

DAY 6: **He's Got You Covered!**

But I trust in you, O LORD; I say, "You are my God." My times are in your hands; deliver me from my enemies and from those who pursue me. Let your face shine on your servant; save me in your unfailing love (Psalm 31:14-16).

God created us to love life. We don't want to think of dying, even when we know for sure that we will spend eternity in heaven with Jesus. It's natural to cling to life. But we also need to realize that our "times are in His hands." God is the One who will decide our moment to die and we can trust Him that it will be the right moment. Sometimes we face situations where we are in great danger or fear, and there is nothing we can do to save ourselves. In those times, we must remember that God really is in control and that His love is unfailing.

When you are in a crisis, go ahead and ask Him to deliver you. He still performs miracles. But if the miracle doesn't come, remember that your times are in His hands and He won't drop you. What do you need to trust God for now?

DEVOTIONALS

DAY 7: **Life is Hard ... Find Joy**

Though the fig tree does not bud and there are no grapes on the vines, though the olive crop fails and the fields produce no food, though there are no sheep in the pen and no cattle in the stalls, yet I will rejoice in the LORD, I will be joyful in God my Savior (Habakkuk 3:17-18).

Standing up for what is right may lead to consequences that are tough to take. We'd like all these stories of courage to end in glorious victory. In fairy tales, the knight in shining armor sets out to right a great wrong, slays the dragon, and then heads home rejoicing with a fine palomino and a bag of gold. In reality, God sometimes gives us a task to do, but when we do it, no one thanks us. In fact, they might be upset. We stand up for truth, and instead of being promoted, we get fired. We help someone in trouble and instead of being praised, people drop us like hot potatoes for fear they will have to get involved. Being serious about following Christ might cost more than you wanted. You might sacrifice success, or fame, or pleasure, or friendships, or even your life. But in the end, Jesus will be worth it. Even if it seems that material prosperity has passed you by, you can rejoice—simply because you know the Creator of the universe intimately.

When have you found it hardest to rejoice in the Lord? Why do you think this was? Ask God to increase your joy in Him because of Who He is and because of His unfailing love for you.

18

DEVOTIONALS

DAY 8: **I'll Knock Your Teeth Out!**

But I tell you, do not resist an evil person. If someone strikes you on the right cheek, turn to him the other also (Matthew 5:39).

In the Old Testament times, God set limits on revenge. People were prone to say, "You chipped my tooth! Just for that, I'm going to punch out all your teeth!" But God set a limit, saying essentially, "Eye for eye, tooth for tooth—no more." But later in the New Testament, Jesus went to the heart of the matter, and gave us a different code. He said essentially, "Let it go." If someone offends you, let it go. Leave punishing that person up to God. He is completely just and anyone who sins will be fairly dealt with.

Jesus isn't talking about just our petty fights with people we care about. He said, "an evil person." This means that when a jealous co-worker tries to get you into trouble with the boss or someone cheats you out of money, you are not to retaliate. We can defend ourselves from false accusations, but we can't do it by destroying our accusers. We must leave them in God's hands.

With whom might you need to "turn the other cheek" right now? What anger, bitterness, or resentment do you need to let go of?

_____

_____

_____

_____

_____

_____

_____

_____

_____

_____

_____

_____

_____

DEVOTIONALS

DAY 9: **This World Is Not My Home**

For me to live is Christ and to die is gain. If I am to go on living in the body, this will mean fruitful labor for me. Yet what shall I choose? I do not know! I am torn between the two: I desire to depart and be with Christ, which is better by far ... (Philippians 1:21-23).

No one likes to imagine his or her whole life going up in smoke. We don't like to think about persecution, or dying for our beliefs. Hopefully, we won't have to face any of those things. But even if we are protected from major catastrophes, there will be disappointments and dry, difficult times. There is only one thing that will carry us through hard times, and leave our souls intact—a relationship with Jesus Christ.

Paul wasn't trying to sound melodramatic when he claimed: "For me to live is Christ." He really meant it. When your relationship with God is central in your life, He will give you previews of heaven, where you'll be in open communications with Him. As you learn to love Him and feel at home with Him, the time will come when you can say, "I'm glad to stay, but I'll be even more glad to go."

Do you think you could say this now? Why or why not? Ask God to develop greater connection and intimacy with Christ in your life. Write your prayer down now.

_____

_____

_____

_____

_____

_____

_____

_____

_____

_____

_____

DEVOTIONALS

DAY 10: **Your Crown of Life**

Do not be afraid of what you are about to suffer. I tell you, the devil will put some of you in prison to test you, and you will suffer persecution for ten days. Be faithful, even to the point of death, and I will give you the crown of life (Revelation 2:10).

It can be difficult to consistently stand up for what is right. At first, when we are full of enthusiasm, it's great. But as the heat turns up and fewer people want to stick with us, we may want to quit, too. It will seem much easier to drift with the crowd for a while. We don't want to appear weird or make others think Christ-followers are fanatics. Above all, we don't want anything to hurt. We work hard to avoid pain.

Be encouraged. God knows we feel this way and He has promised to help us. Not only that, He has promised that those who stick it out will receive His reward. When we grow tired, we have to remind ourselves that His approval is going to be worth more than a little rest or freedom from pain now.

What trials or storms do you particularly fear? For what pain or suffering do you need God's perspective right now?

_____

_____

_____

_____

_____

_____

_____

_____

_____

_____

_____

_____

_____

_____

Great Walls of Fire ... Finding Confidence in Adversity (Shadrach, Meshach, and Abednego)

Daniel 3:1-30

People in our society learn about fire and fire safety at a very young age. We give our toddlers toy fire trucks. School children tour fire stations with their classes. In elementary school, we hold fire drills. We purchase fire extinguishers and smoke alarms. In any hotel, the back of the door has a sign that reads, "What To Do In Case Of A Fire."

Today we are going to think about fire. We're not talking about fires that destroy homes or forests, but spiritual fires that we face. The personal crises we encounter are like fire to our souls. When these great walls of fire surround us and they seem to be closing in around us, what can we do? Who do we turn to?

START IT UP

We humans have conflicting feelings about fire: we need it and fear it at the same time. Fire in the fireplace is cheering and comforting; fire out of control consumes and destroys.

1. **Have you ever had dreams about fires? If so, what key details do you remember about them?**

2. Today, how do you feel about fire? Does it fascinate or frighten you? What might have influenced your attitude toward fire?

TALK IT UP

The Bible tells us the story of three men who experienced literal "great walls of fire." Through their experience, we can glean five "fireproof formulas" for dealing with the frightening, and soul-searing problems that attack us.

To set the stage, we need to go back in history. In 605 B.C., King Nebuchadnezzar took the reins of Babylon. Nebuchadnezzar was a proud man, and a powerful one. One of his conquests was the land of Israel. He subdued the nation and carried off its treasures. He also picked out the brightest, most intelligent young men from the best families in Judah. He took them back to Babylon, educated them in the Babylonian culture, and put them into top positions in his administration. Three of those young men were Shadrach, Meshach, and Abednego. King Nebuchadnezzar eventually gave these young men administrative responsibility over the province of Babylon.

Read Daniel 3:1-12

We all cheer when we see how the three young men refused to bow to Nebuchadnezzar's statue. You might assume these heroes would get away with disobeying the king because they were obeying God. But something happened that still happens today. Some verbal flamethrowers came onto the scene. They went to the king and accused the Jews of refusing to bow to Nebuchadnezzar's image. (Verbal arsonists always work behind your back.) They didn't come face to face with Shadrach, Meshach, and Abednego. Instead, they crept around and set a fire by tattletaling. If you are in any position of leadership, get ready for the verbal arsonists because they are lurking everywhere.

Read Daniel 3:13-18

Fireproof Formula 1: Rise Above the Verbal Flamethrowers.

If we want to put out the fires in our lives, we have to rise above the verbal flamethrowers. Shadrach, Meshach, and Abednego were able to rise above them because they had proper priorities. When your top priority is God's approval, you are confident. You don't need everyone else's approval. Every time you return fire with fire you will be disappointed. You slide down to the flamethrower's level. It's human nature to want revenge for those who hurt us, but if our priorities are straight, we can be confident, serene, and secure. We can leave revenge in God's hands and trust that even being hit by the flamethrowers will be used for good in God's grand scheme.

Fireproof Formula 2: Walk Through "Fiery Furnaces" with Confidence.

Shadrach, Meshach, and Abednego knew the cost of their obedience. They knew that refusing to bow to the statue would cost them their careers and probably their lives. Yet, they were confident that obeying God was the right thing to do and they need not worry about the future. They obeyed God and left their welfare in God's hands. It's important to notice that they reflected confidence, not cockiness. They were not exhibiting bravado, nor were they sassing Nebuchadnezzar to cover up their fear of punishment. Their confidence came directly from their knowledge of God. They didn't say, "Israel's God," or "a God," or just "God." They said, "Our God can save us." They could say "Our God" with confidence because they knew Him personally. Confidence in God comes from a personal relationship with Him.

3. **What are some examples of real-life crises that we could identify as "fiery furnaces"? How would personal knowledge of God's character help a person deal with these things?**

Fireproof Formula 3: Don't Compromise When the Fire Flares Up.

Shadrach, Meshach, and Abednego were confident of God's power and His commands. They were tranquil because they were obedient—not because they knew how it would turn out. They didn't know whether God would rescue them or not. They were in a fearful place and if anyone ever had an excuse to compromise, they did. They could easily have said, "Well, true worship comes from the heart, right? So if we bow down, but we're not worshipping in our hearts, then it doesn't count. We can do this; it isn't such a big deal." They could easily have saved their own lives. But they didn't allow circumstances to compromise their worship. Instead they said, "Yeah, we might die. But that doesn't really matter. I've got to do what God says, no matter what."

We all love stories with happy endings, but many times God doesn't miraculously save His obedient servants. Perhaps obeying God could mean sacrificing your career. You may lose friends or reputation if you follow God's commands and you may never be justified. Fire might consume your "success" as this world defines it. Sometimes Christians even die because of their refusal to compromise.

4. **Where are you most tempted to compromise? Can you behave differently with different groups of people without compromising? How far can you go without being disobedient?**

5. **Why doesn't God always rescue His people from the fiery furnaces of life? Is it still worth following Him without a guarantee that He will rescue you? Why?**

Read Daniel 3:19-30

Fireproof Formula 4: Grasp God's Hand as You Walk Through the Fire.

Nebuchadnezzar was watching for his rebellious servants to burn. As he watched, he witnessed something incredible! The three young men were walking around in a furnace so hot that the guards who threw them in had been killed. Incredibly, He also saw a fourth person walking through the fire with them. Many scholars believe this fourth person was Jesus Himself making an appearance before He came to earth as the God-man in Bethlehem.

We are on life's stage when we are going through a fire. Our audience may be someone who wants to see us burn. Or it might be someone desperately hoping for a glimpse of God, hoping to see Him rescue us from the flames. If we respond by reaching for God's hand, the spectators will see what Nebuchadnezzar saw. They will see Jesus walking through the flames with us. They will see that we do not burn, and some of them will say, "That person has something I want."

Just like the fire in the furnace burnt off the ropes that bound Shadrach, Meshach, and Abednego, God sometimes allows fires in our lives in order to burn away things that hold us captive. God is not "out to get us;" He wants to free us for His purposes. Scripture promises us that God will be with us when we pass through fiery trials. No one likes the fiery times but God is present with us teaching us invaluable lessons. Afterwards, we will be able to say: "I've learned more in the fire than anywhere else. It was tough, but I wouldn't trade it. I know Him in such a different, deeper way now."

God works on us like a master goldsmith. A goldsmith heats his metal to the melting point. As it melts, the heavy gold sinks to the bottom and the scum of dirt and impurities rise to the top. Then the goldsmith carefully skims the dross off the top, leaving the pure gold in the crucible. He knows that the gold is pure when he can see his own reflection in its molten surface. The Lord uses a similar process in our lives. As the heat increases in our fiery trials, the impurities and dirt rise to the top, and He skims them off. And as He works with us melting, refining, and cleansing, God is looking for one thing. He is looking to see His own reflection in our lives.

6. **What character qualities are produced by "fire" in our lives? Why do you think these particular qualities come out of "fiery" experiences?**

7. **When have you been in the furnace with God? What did you learn through the experience? Do you think it brought you closer to reflecting His image?**

Fireproof Formula 5: Recognize a Promotion Awaits You Beyond the Fire.

After Nebuchadnezzar saw the three young men pass through the fire unharmed, he was impressed both by their character and by the power of the God they served. His immediate reaction was not only to restore their positions, but also to promote them. This is also a picture of what happens when we successfully pass through fires in our lives. God is waiting to promote us. This word "promote" is not a promise of prosperity. God doesn't promise to make us rich or famous; He promises to make us more and more like Him. You may not hear anything more about your promotion until you get to heaven. But think about it this way: If you hear the God of all creation say to you, personally, "Well done! You have been a faithful servant, and I am pleased with you," won't that be amazing?

8. **What is this world's definition of success? What do you think God's definition of success is? Which definition do you really live by?**

9. **Read Daniel 3:28 again. Do you think anyone would be able to say this about you? What things in our lives might come under the category of "serving" or "worshiping" another god?**

LIFT IT UP

Every one of us will walk through a "fiery furnace" of some kind—an experience that will test our faith and either burn out impurities or burn us up. Sometimes it will seem like we can't make it through without being wounded forever. But remember this: even if you lose your career, your home, your friends, or your life but you keep your grip on God's hand, you will be victorious. The question to ask is not, "Will I win? Will people realize that I'm right? Will those verbal arsonists have to eat dirt?" but "Am I obeying God? Am I doing the job He gave me to do?" Ultimately, we have to leave the consequences of our obedience in God's hands.

10. How can this group pray for you as you are walking through the fires of life?

11. What results of previous fires can you thank God for?

Take time to pray together for each other and the fires that each one currently faces

My Prayer Needs:

_____

_____

_____

_____

My Group's Prayer Needs:

_____

_____

_____

_____

_____

_____

_____

_____

DEVOTIONALS

DAY 1: **Life's Earthquakes**

God is our refuge and strength, an ever-present help in trouble. Therefore we will not fear, though the earth give way and the mountains fall into the heart of the sea, though its waters roar and foam and the mountains quake with their surging (Psalm 46:1-3).

Life is a mixed bag. Some of it is fun, some is boring, some is sweet, and some of it is just plain scary. Throughout our lives, each of us will face times of uncertainty or even disaster. We will be faced with crises we don't feel capable of handling, or times when all the available choices seem risky. But no matter what happens, we can be sure that God is still in control. We can live life with courage because we know God has His hand on us. We'll never be fear-free; danger and uncertainty will always be with us. But remember this: life may be a big risk, but we have a bigger God.

What situation in your life seems like "mountains falling" on you? Write these things down, and then look at the list. Have you asked for God's help to handle each of these things?

DAY 2: **A Powerful Weakling**

But he [Jesus] said to me [Paul], "My grace is sufficient for you, for my power is made perfect in weakness." Therefore I will boast all the more gladly about my weaknesses, so that Christ's power may rest on me (2 Corinthians 12:9).

Intellectual knowledge of God's power and actually feeling secure can be two very different things. We'd rather God infuse us with a jolt of super-courage. But God doesn't work that way. He knows our weaknesses and uses them to draw us close to Him. When we see just how far we fall short, we realize how much we need Him. Remember, God wants relationship and communication with us. Every day, and every hour as we face temptations and trials He wants us to say, "I am weak. I can't do this by myself. I am putting my hand in yours. Help me."

What is your biggest weakness? When particularly do you find yourself struggling with this? Ask God to give you strength to do what is right the next time you face this temptation. God builds our strength one victory at a time.

DEVOTIONALS

DAY 3: **The Real Enemy**

I tell you, my friends, do not be afraid of those who kill the body and after that can do no more. But I will show you whom you should fear: Fear him who, after killing of the body, has power to throw you into hell. Yes, I tell you fear him (Luke 12:4-5).

Many people hesitate to follow Christ because they fear persecution. They don't want to lose careers, prestige, or "getting my own way." They don't realize that they fear the wrong enemy. Losing a little money, a little recognition or even losing your life is nothing compared to losing your soul.

Too often, Christ-followers face the same fears. We don't want to risk our jobs, reputations, or security. We are afraid of those who can kill the body without realizing that we are looking at the wrong enemies. Do you want to stand before Christ when your life is done and acknowledge that you cared more about your financial portfolio or your comfort than about obeying Him?

Write down the three things you fear most in this world. How do you think these fears might be keeping you from effectively and passionately following God?

_____

_____

_____

_____

_____

_____

_____

_____

_____

_____

_____

_____

_____

_____

_____

_____

DAY 4: **What Am I Worth?**

Are not five sparrows sold for two pennies? Yet not one of them is forgotten by God. Indeed the very hairs of your head are all numbered. Don't be afraid; you are worth more than many sparrows (Luke 12:6-7).

One reason we struggle with fear is that we're not sure God will rescue us. We are afraid we will be defeated or destroyed. But God isn't some "Man Upstairs" who might happen to notice you if you are extraordinarily evil or especially good. He made each one of us and knows all that happens to us, down to the smallest detail. He notices when one eyelash falls out—so, do you think He's not going to help when you are in trouble?

What has God done for you to let you know how much you are worth to Him? What doubts do you still have about your worth to God? Take those to Him in prayer and allow Him to show you the Truth.

DAY 5: **Strap On Your Armor**

Therefore put on the full armor of God, so that when the day of evil comes, you may be able to stand your ground, and after you have done everything, to stand. Stand firm then, with the belt of truth buckled around your waist, with the breastplate of righteousness in place, and with your feet fitted with the readiness that comes from the gospel of peace (Ephesians 6:13-14).

Life is made more difficult because Satan is out to get us. We are not struggling simply with natural disasters, or bad habits, or crabby people. Satan uses hardships to drag us down into sin. We are in a spiritual battle, and most of us haven't even realized it. But God doesn't leave us to fight alone. He has promised to be with us and has provided us with "armor" to wear that will protect us from Satan's attacks. Paul uses different pieces of armor as metaphors for the protection God gives us. The belt holds all the rest of the armor in place in the same way that the truth of the gospel holds our faith in place. A breastplate protects the vital organs from attack just as righteousness will protect our hearts from being corrupted.

Read the next few verses of Ephesians 6. How would you translate each of these armor metaphors? Which piece of armor do you feel like you are missing? What will help you to strap it on?

_____

_____

_____

_____

_____

_____

_____

_____

_____

_____

_____

_____

DEVOTIONALS

DAY 6: **Called to Hate?**

If anyone comes to me and does not hate his father and mother, his wife and children, his brothers and sisters—yes, even his own life—he cannot be my disciple (Luke 14:26).

At first glance, this verse seems almost incomprehensible. Could Jesus have really said this? Is this the same Jesus who said, "Love your enemies," and "the one who hates has committed murder in his heart"? Yes, Jesus really did say this, and He really meant it. He used strong language to make His point because it is such an important one. Our devotion to Him should be so strong that if we had to make a choice, we would choose Him over those closest to us.

Most people are attracted to the love passages of scripture for a very good reason. God is love and He wants people to experience and understand His love. Our culture really gets off base on this issue. "Oh, I can't say that person's lifestyle is wrong. That wouldn't be loving." "I can't stand up for God in this situation; I might hurt someone's feelings." If we are really following Christ, our lives will be overflowing with love for the people around us. But at the same time, we may have to stand for a conviction and risk upsetting those we love. Unless we are willing to risk human disapproval to follow Christ, we aren't really serious about loving Him. Love isn't just "warm fuzzies." Love must be based on truth.

Write down three things you think are important enough to take a stand on. Why are these things so important to you?

_____

_____

_____

_____

_____

_____

_____

_____

_____

_____

_____

_____

_____

DAY 7: **Worthy of Christ**

Whatever happens, conduct yourselves in a manner worthy of the gospel of Christ. Then, whether I come and see you or only hear about you in my absence, I will know that you stand firm in one spirit, contending as one man for the faith of the gospel without being frightened in any way by those who oppose you (Philippians 1:27-28).

Often it takes more courage to remain faithful in day-to-day life than in great acts of daring or endurance. When your friends say, "Don't you get to have any fun?" the temptation to join them can be very real. It takes real strength to say, "No," when your boss asks you to cut an ethical corner. It takes courage when a teenager won't let her best friend cheat from her exam, even if it means she's mad for the rest of the year. The ridicule of our peers is difficult to bear. But when you are in these situations and wondering if "just one time" doesn't matter, ask yourself one question: "Am I acting in a manner worthy of the gospel of Christ?"

Write down three day to say situations that often tempt you. Sometimes just acknowledging the reality of the struggle helps us find the courage to remain faithful.

DEVOTIONALS

DAY 8: **You're Under Surveillance**

Do everything without complaining or arguing, so that you may become blameless and pure, children of God without fault in a crooked and depraved generation, in which you shine like stars in the universe ... (Philippians 2:14-15).

Not only is God keeping track of what you are doing, but the whole world is also watching your claim to follow Christ. We know that we damage Jesus' cause if we murder or commit adultery, abuse children or rob banks. But most of us forget that people will notice if we are constantly complaining or mean-spirited, or if we argue and push to get our way. They will look at us and say, "Man, Christians sure are negative!" or "Church people are always fighting among themselves."

What kind of image do you think your neighbors have of you? Ask God to reveal to you what areas of your life need to be cleaned up.

DAY 9: **Courage Is Catching**

After he said this, he took some bread and gave thanks to God in front of them all. Then he broke it and began to eat. They were all encouraged and ate some food themselves (Acts 27:35-36).

Paul was in a situation where anyone would excuse him for feeling defeated. He had been attacked by a mob, arrested, thrown in jail on false charges, and kept there for two years. Now he was being taken as a prisoner to Rome where he would be tried before Caesar. He didn't know whether he would be pardoned or executed when he arrived. Now, his ship was caught in a violent storm and was breaking apart in the wind and waves. Paul probably expected to be thrown into the sea by the guards. No one would risk letting a prisoner escape. But in the midst of all this, Paul did not lose heart. From a human perspective, everything was wrong, but Paul had God's assurance that all would be well, and Paul believed Him. Here he was, a prisoner, probably soaking wet after two weeks of wild weather on the Mediterranean, in danger of drowning or execution ... and he cheerfully tells them all to eat because they would all be saved. They had no reason to believe him, but courage is catching. Paul was serenely confident because he knew the God he served.

Is there someone in your life that needs to be encouraged? How could you do this? Pray and ask God to give them the strength they need.

DEVOTIONALS

DAY 10: **Equilibrium**

Do not be anxious about anything, but in everything, by prayer and petition, with thanksgiving, present your requests to God. And the peace of God, which transcends all understanding, will guard your hearts and your minds in Christ Jesus (Philippians 4:6).

No matter how overwhelming it seems, no situation is beyond God's help. It is always on His radar; He's never caught off-guard. When we are in trouble, God wants us to ask Him for help. He also wants us to thank Him for the good He brings out of a mess. When we realize that all things will work together for good for those who love the Lord (Romans 8:28), we can meet life with unnatural calmness and peace. We can trust that nothing is wasted with God.

Write down your requests and take them to God. Look back at these in a few weeks or months and see how God has worked in your life.

Lion Food ...
Developing Courage (Daniel)

Daniel 1:8-17; 6:3-28; Joshua 1:8-9

We all want courage but few of us possess it. We excuse ourselves, saying, "Courage is something for extraordinary people, those human mutations, not for ordinary people like me." That thinking is false. The longer you live, the more you realize how much courage it takes just to live a normal life.

Choices bombard us in rapid-fire succession. We can choose to stand for courage or cower. We can say, "I'm going to make a difference" or "I'm going to retreat into my shell." "I'm going to follow God's lead even though it seems strange and countercultural" or "I'm going to take the easy way out." Most of us make decisions so quickly that we are oblivious to the process. We just go with the flow and let life happen. We miss the fact that God wants all of us, even ordinary you, to be people of courage.

START IT UP

The most courageous acts are not necessarily accompanied by brave thoughts, but by a good deal of fear and "just doing what had to be done."

1. When you were growing up, what were you most afraid of?

2. Identify a real life person whose courage you particularly admire. What makes this person especially courageous to you?

TALK IT UP

Courage is a quality we instinctively admire. Most of us dream of doing some spectacular act of bravery and being the hero of the day. But courage is not a one-dimensional character quality. It's not only the spectacular act of saving children from a burning house or rescuing someone from an enraged grizzly bear. Courage is multi-dimensional; it should be present in all we do. Day to day courage doesn't necessarily get the press clippings or the praise. But day to day courage makes us strong, and builds us into the people that God intended.

In this session we will examine the life of Daniel, the Hebrew captive in Babylon, whose life is a full-color, three-dimensional illustration of courage.

Last time, we discussed King Nebuchadnezzar and how his armies took over Jerusalem and the kingdom of Judah. Besides stealing all the gold and the treasures of the temple of God, the Babylonians also captured the brightest and best of their young people. Daniel was among those taken captive. Daniel was probably about 16 when he was transported from his home in Judah to the decadent city of Babylon. He was placed in the king's elite school, to be trained in the language and culture of the Babylonians and be prepared to enter the king's service.

Spiritual Courage

Read Daniel 1:8-17

The first dimension of courage we need to examine is spiritual courage. Our culture needs people of spiritual courage these days. But how is this episode in Daniel 1 talking about spiritual courage? The cafeteria food at the king's school doesn't seem like such a big deal, does it? It seems like a little thing to make an issue of. But wait—there is more to this story.

Daniel and his friends were not just health food fanatics, objecting to a diet high in fat and cholesterol. They held a deeper, more spiritual reason for refusing the king's food. When God rescued the Hebrew people from slavery, He created a nation set apart for Him. The laws He gave them were not only about moral behavior, but also meant to emphasize the uniqueness of belonging to God alone. These laws included dietary restrictions. Daniel knew that the king's food did not fulfill the laws God had given them. And because he was committed to following God, he chose to reject the "unclean" food.

We might think Daniel could have compromised here. He was a captive and not in charge of the kitchens. Surely God would have overlooked Daniel ignoring the diet. Daniel was 500 miles from Jerusalem, with every reason to adopt the pagan Babylonian culture. But he did not choose the way of compromise. He chose the way of courage. If you will develop courage, it starts in bite-sized chunks.

SESSION THREE

Living life as a Christ-follower takes courage. Many times God's leading in our lives seems difficult, and even counter-cultural. It takes courage to step out and do what God asks; it may even seem weird or unnecessary from our point of view. You may find yourself doing something you think is crazy, but you trust God even if you can't see the outcome beforehand. Daniel lived this kind of courageous life. He didn't understand the reasons for God's requirements. He didn't know how the situation would turn out, but he still obeyed God courageously. He was willing to risk being different.

> **3. What are things God sometimes asks us to do that might seem "weird" to the people around us?**

Ethical Courage

Sixty years later, Daniel was still in Babylon when a new king came on the scene—Darius the Mede. Darius was really impressed with Daniel, because he recognized the difference in Daniel's life.

Read Daniel 6:3-9

Read Daniel 6:4 again, and this time substitute your own name. Could someone say this about you? Or would they say, "We found major, moral problems and ethical foul-ups in this person's life"? We need ethical courage in the marketplace today. You are talking to a client on the phone and you say, "It cost us $2,500," but in actuality you know you paid $1,800 for it. "The check is in the mail," but the check hasn't been cut. "Yeah, I talked to him yesterday about this," and the truth is you hadn't talked to this man in a year. Do you live an ethically courageous life?

It's time for us to stop living a "go with the flow" mentality, living a life without moral courage. It's time to say, "I'm going to live like Daniel, modeling a life of ethical courage." We can be courageous people who will not be moved—people with ethical courage.

> **4. What are some areas of your life today where you need to maintain and strengthen your ethical courage?**

Relational Courage

Read Daniel 6:10-28

Daniel also possessed a third dimension of courage: relational courage. He stood up to King Darius—someone he was close to. Despite their relationship, Daniel still didn't hesitate to obey God. He would not say, "Well, you know, Darius is my friend. If I force the issue and make him follow through on his edict, he'll be hurt, too. He will think I'm some kind of fanatic; he will be turned off and then not be interested in following my God. I can just lay low for a month, and it will all blow over. My relationship with Darius will be intact, and I can pick up with God later." Instead, he took the hard path.

5. **How can we show relational courage in our marriages? With our children? With our parents? With our friends?**

6. **How could showing relational courage actually draw people to God?**

Developing Courage

We all want to be courageous people who stand up for God and make a difference. How do we do it? First, we have to **eat spiritual food.** Spiritual food includes reading and studying the Bible, as well as talking to God in prayer. Daniel took in three square spiritual meals a day. He knew that his spiritual diet was important and he stayed connected to God. Too many times, we do "drive-through prayers." We say, "Yes, God, this is me—I'd like a blessing, some guidance, and a side order of encouragement, thank you." Then we expect God to say, "That'll be $7.25, drive up to the second window to pick up your order." We are settling for appetizers instead of going for the full-course meal.

Read Joshua 1:8

7. **What does it mean to meditate on the Bible (Book of the Law)? What is the result of meditating on God's Word?**

Spiritual depth happens when we talk about God's Word, think about it, and then obey it. Great preaching and Bible study is not informational; it's transformational. We tend to walk around saying, "I am getting really spiritually deep, I finally figured out the complex aqueduct system during the reign of Solomon." That's deep? That's doing God's work? It's interesting, but that's not spiritual depth. We need to know the Bible, but we also have to live it. Thinking and talking about God's Word is like eating spiritual food—it provides spiritual calories—the energy to put it into action.

Read Joshua 1:9

The second step is *realizing that courage is standard equipment* for people who follow Christ; it's not optional. Most of us have a variety of "collapsible" courage. We take our courage out when it is convenient or when those around us are supporting and encouraging us. But then when pressure begins to squeeze us, we fold up our courage and blend into the background.

8. **God's faithfulness in the past helps us to have courage today. What reason do you have to be courageous today?**

Third, we have to *face our "lions."* Daniel faced those snaggle-toothed, bad-breathed, 1200 pound kings of the jungle breathing down his neck for hours. Do you know what courageous people are? Courageous people are ordinary people who face their fears. Courageous people face the lions even though they are scared. If you don't face your lions, the lions will get bigger and bigger until one day they will rip you apart. If you face the lions there might be sorrow and maybe even defeat, but ultimately you will see victory. If you rely on God and face those fears, every battle you win will be like rungs on a ladder. You climb higher and higher upward on that wall of courage.

Fourth, we must limit our exposure to cowardly people. This doesn't mean you should never associate with those who lack courage—you'd have to live on a desert island. But it does mean that you need relationships with people who will encourage you, people who are strong and who are not afraid to stand for God.

LIFT IT UP

When we look at ourselves and see the timid, weak-spined creatures that we are when under stress, developing courage seems like a daunting task. We have great intentions; we think "high thoughts" and tell ourselves that next time it will be different. But so often, when that defining moment comes, our courage collapses.

Remember, becoming people of courage is not a one-time event. Real courage is lived out in the little everyday decisions. When we practice showing courage in our everyday relationships, in our businesses, and in our spiritual lives, then when the big tests hit us, our "courage muscles" are already toned.

9. In what area of your life do you most need to develop your courage?

10. Think about your relationships. Do you have some courageous friends who build you up? Where could you look for some people like this?

Take time to pray together to encourage each other in the areas where courage is lacking.

My Prayer Needs:

_____

_____

_____

My Group's Prayer Needs:

_____

_____

_____

_____

_____

_____

_____

_____

_____

_____

DEVOTIONALS

DAY 1: **The Starting Point**

The fear of the LORD is the beginning of wisdom; all who follow his precepts have good understanding. To him belongs eternal praise (Psalm 111:10).

We are constantly making decisions. We get up in the morning and decide which clothes to put on. We decide what to eat, in what order we do our work, what house to buy, where to go to church and whom to marry. Whether we choose cereal or a bagel for breakfast probably won't affect anyone. But some of our decisions are life changing and it is these decisions we often make the biggest mess of. We desperately need wisdom and insight regarding how we live our lives. And there is only one place to start.

Fearing God means holding Him in reverent awe, respecting His power and authority as well as marveling at His love, mercy, and grace. To fear God is to recognize that He's in charge and that we are not. That's the first step toward wisdom

Do you fear God? Write down three ways that fear of God might be obvious in your life or might need to be strengthened.

DEVOTIONALS

DAY 2: **Dialing Up the Wisdom Line**

If any of you lacks wisdom, he should ask God, who gives generously to all without finding fault, and it will be given to him (James 1:5).

Even though we do fear God, many of us continue to flounder in a sea of indecision. We know who God is and we believe in His Word. But we rarely communicate with Him. We don't know what to do because we never asked Him for direction. The Apostle James encourages us to communicate with God, because God wants to communicate with us.

Wisdom from God usually doesn't mean step-by-step instructions. We'd prefer that, but God allows us to use the intelligence and common sense He gave us. Receiving wisdom from God isn't like gazing into a crystal ball. Rather, it is God helping us to see life from His point of view, so that we can make wise decisions

What situations are you in now where you feel the need for God's wisdom? Make a list of these things, and then specifically ask God to give you the wisdom you need in each situation. Look back on this list in a few weeks or months and see how God has answered your prayers.

DEVOTIONALS

DAY 3: **Don't Hang Up Yet**

But when he asks, he must believe and not doubt, because he who doubts is like a wave of the sea, blown and tossed by the wind. That man should not think he will receive anything from the Lord; he is a double-minded man, unstable in all he does (James 1:6-7).

"I don't think God will bother to answer me—He never does. There isn't really any point in asking." "I don't really believe in God, but I'll just pray to satisfy this friend who thinks I should. After all, it's harmless enough." "What if God didn't really mean what He said? What if He won't answer me after all?" " I've decided prayer doesn't work. I asked for four different things this week and didn't get a single one."

If we are asking God for wisdom or anything else as an experiment, our prayers probably will not be answered. Prayer isn't a coin we put into the divine vending machine to get a certain product. Prayer is about communication. That's why James says, "Ask," rather than "recite these words three times, facing east." God is real. He is personal and He has promised that He will answer in the right way. Experimental prayer isn't communication; it is an attempt to manipulate God.

Do you think that you pray more often with faith or with doubt? What makes you doubtful? Ask God to help you handle these things with faith.

_____

_____

_____

_____

_____

_____

_____

_____

_____

_____

DEVOTIONALS

DAY 4: **What Does God Want?**

He has showed you, O man, what is good. And what does the LORD require of you? To act justly and to love mercy and to walk humbly with your God (Micah 6:8).

Every Christ-follower has wondered, "What is God's will for my life?" God does have plans for us. He has given each of us our specific talents and resources for use in His Kingdom. What we do matters to God. But we tend to look at this issue backwards. We worry and fret because we don't feel that God has given us clear-cut answers to our questions when we have neglected the clear instructions He already gave us. Each of us knows exactly what the foundation of "God's will for my life" is. God requires us to be morally upright, kind, and gentle. Above all, we are to possess an attitude of humility before God. The good news is that when we act on what we already know to do, the specifics will fall into place. When we are in tune with God we can look at our decisions and answer the question, "Is this what God wants me to do?"

Describe what "walking humbly with God" might look like in your life. Ask God to develop more of this quality in your life.

_____

_____

_____

_____

_____

_____

_____

_____

_____

_____

_____

_____

_____

_____

DEVOTIONALS

DAY 5: **Let's Step Outside**

Do nothing out of selfish ambition or vain conceit, but in humility consider others better than yourselves (Philippians 2:3).

We don't say it this bluntly, but most of us consider ourselves to be pretty special. The fact is—we are. Every single one of us is unique and beloved by God. The problems arise when we consider own "specialness" a bit more "special" than anyone else. The obvious way we display this selfishness is in pride and vanity. We subtly lord it over other people, trying to prove to them that we are better. We turn all our energy inward, focusing on "great, big, beautiful Me." The second way is a little less obvious. We indulge in an inverted selfishness by feeling inferior to others. We turn all our energy inward, focusing on "poor, little, sad Me." Over and over again, our bad decisions can be traced to one source: selfishness. God has called us to break out of the mold and turn our personal attention outward. Once we recognize our own "specialness," He wants us to step outside ourselves and recognize and affirm the "specialness" of others.

What are some practical ways that you could show that you consider your spouse (friend, parent, co-worker, room-mate, or family member) better than yourself?

DEVOTIONALS

DAY 6: **Wake Up!**

How long will you lie there, you sluggard? When will you get up from your sleep? A little sleep, a little slumber, a little folding of the hands to rest—and poverty will come on you like a bandit and scarcity like an armed man (Proverbs 6:9-11).

Most of us have tried this approach to difficult decisions. It's easy and it comes naturally to us: Just do nothing and maybe it will go away. In fact, if we do nothing, moments of decision will pass—and they may be gone forever. Repeatedly, when we look back from a disaster trying to understand where we made a bad decision, we realize that we made no decision at all. We just drifted into it. Avoiding decisions may be easy right now, but it isn't in the long run. If we let life happen to us, by default we end up with nothing to show for our time on earth.

What kind of life will you have to show when you meet Jesus face to face? Write down two things that you really want to accomplish. Then write down the first step toward each of these things. When will you begin?

_____

_____

_____

_____

_____

_____

_____

_____

_____

_____

_____

_____

_____

_____

_____

DEVOTIONALS

DAY 7: **Slide On By**

A priest happened to be going down the same road, and when he saw the man, he passed by on the other side (Luke 10:31).

Jesus often told stories to teach truth. This verse comes from the story he told of a man who was traveling to the city of Jericho. He was robbed, beaten senseless, and left for dead on the side of the road. He was lying right by the highway, so of course, people soon were passing by. The first person to notice the guy in the ditch was a priest, and this priest did an incredible thing. He saw this man dying and didn't even stop for a closer look. He just crossed the road and hurried on. He was probably thinking, "Well, that is not my job. I'm not a paramedic, and I don't know how to do CPR. Somebody else will stop and help him. I have to keep moving, I have a meeting to attend."

It's easy to be appalled at this priest's reaction. After all, he was supposed to be a servant of God. How could he be so heartless as to leave that poor man there? The fact is that we act just like that priest, over and over again. How many times have you decided "not to get involved" because you thought something looked a bit uncomfortable? How many times have you seen something unjust or unkind happen, and said, "Well, it's none of my business. I'll just pretend I didn't see that"?

In what situations might you have "walked by on the other side" when you could have helped? Ask God to give you His heart and eyes for the needs of others.

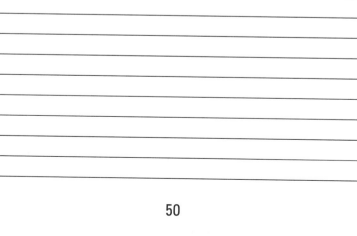

DEVOTIONALS

DAY 8: **Helping Jesus Personally**

I tell you the truth, whatever you did not do for one of the least of these, you did not do for me [Jesus] (Matthew 25:45).

It is popular today to say, "As long as no one is hurt, anything goes." We justify our actions saying that as long as our decisions don't harm others, no one, not even God, has the right to care what we do. We think our freedom is our inalienable right.

While we all know it's sin to make decisions to hurt others, God also calls it sin when we don't make a decision to help others. Living a self-centered life is simply not acceptable. God doesn't call us to be harmless "nothings." He wants us to be helpful, active, useful "somethings." If you heard that Jesus was in prison, would you want to go visit Him? If He was thirsty, would you give Him a drink? If He was hungry, wouldn't you rush to feed Him your very best? We all would. And He said that serving even the most unworthy of the dirtiest people on the streets or in prison counts as though we are serving Him personally.

What people do you know now in your area who are in need (physically, emotionally, spiritually)? What could you do about it?

DEVOTIONALS

DAY 9: **Beefing Up Your "Decision Muscles"**

And we urge you, brothers, warn those who are idle, encourage the timid, help the weak, be patient with everyone. Make sure that nobody pays back wrong for wrong, but always try to be kind to each other and to everyone else. Be joyful always; pray continually; give thanks in all circumstances, for this is God's will for you in Christ Jesus (1 Thessalonians 5:14-18).

God's will isn't very complicated—until we start trying to put it into practice. Seriously attempting to "be patient with everyone" is not an easy task. Every day, every moment, we will have to make the decision again to follow God's way, and not our own. We have to decide to be joyful; decide to give thanks when we don't feel thankful; decide to be kind, generous, and gentle. But when we work on these things, we will make two discoveries. First, with constant use, our "decision muscles" will become stronger and more disciplined. The second discovery is that the more we try to follow God's will as revealed in the Bible, the easier it will be to make our "Defining Moment Decisions" glorify and honor Him.

Read these verses again. What specific situations come to mind for you? Write down at least three that you particularly need help with, and ask God to help you strengthen your "decision muscles."

_____

_____

_____

_____

_____

_____

_____

_____

_____

_____

_____

_____

_____

DEVOTIONALS

DAY 10: **Running Toward the Right Goal**

He who pursues righteousness and love finds life, prosperity and honor (Proverbs 21:21).

What happens to a runner who races for the wrong goal? No matter how fast he is, he never wins the race. The Bible often compares the spiritual life with a race. It takes endurance to run a race, it takes speed and power, but it also takes knowing our goal. It doesn't matter how clever we are, how much money we make, or how carefully we think through our decisions. If we are not aiming for the right goal, we will not cross the finish line with God.

The one who pursues self-gratification, greed, and power will eventually find heartbreak, ruin, and disgrace. If our decisions are based on personal fulfillment, making the most money, or taking revenge on someone, we are going to trip and fall. But if our decisions are based on God, and what He wants, we will find real success and lasting happiness.

What decisions have you made in the last week? What do you think these were based on? Are you running toward the right goal?

_____

_____

_____

_____

_____

_____

_____

_____

_____

_____

_____

_____

_____

_____

Playing With Fire ...
Seizing "Defining Moments" (Lot)

Genesis 13:1-18; 19:1-29; 2 Peter 2:7-

We all face "defining moment" decisions. They come at us in a rapid-fire pace. Some are obviously bold, significant decisions— like who to marry or what career path to choose. But we often make choices without recognizing them as defining moment decisions.

These defining moment decisions yield enormous implications in all of our lives. Decisions we make today greatly influence who we will be tomorrow. Many of us are facing these decisions right now.

START IT UP

Our culture prefers a wide range of choices for everything. We love having options, but keeping up with all these decisions can be overwhelming.

1. **What is the strangest food you have chosen from a salad bar or buffet? Do you choose quickly or do you like to take your time?**

2. **What is a recent decision you are glad you made?**

TALK IT UP

We're going to look at an Old Testament man with an impressive resume. Our man, Lot, was the nephew of Abraham—the man remembered throughout the Bible for his amazing faith. Abraham was fabulously wealthy in his time. He had flocks and herds and servants by the hundreds. Lot's father died while Lot was still young and from that time his uncle, Abraham, looked after him. Abraham must have taught Lot his business skills, because Lot accumulated a fortune of his own.

There came a day when God told Abraham to move. Abraham, being a man of faith, packed his bags and started out. He took all his wealth, his family, and he also took along his nephew Lot. It was like two huge corporations moving together. Naturally in a situation like that you can expect some conflict. This conflict was not between Lot and Abraham, but between their employees.

Where is Your Tent Pitched?

Read Genesis 13:1-13

Abraham was facing a defining moment decision. He had to decide how to deal with the conflict between his and Lot's employees. He made the choice to put family peace above personal gain. He suggested that they go separate ways. Then, even though Abraham had the most seniority, he gave first choice of grazing ground to Lot.

> 3. **What was Lot looking at when he made his decision? What was Abraham looking at? Who got the best deal and why?**

Lot didn't recognize that he was deciding about a defining moment. He didn't realize his choice would affect the rest of his life. Nowhere does Lot say, "Uncle Abraham, give me some advice. What do you think would be the best way to divide the land?" Instead, he thought only of himself and what would be good for his family. Selfish decisions usually lead to destruction, while unselfish decisions usually lead to life. Lot thought only of Lot and, as a result, he messed up. He made a selfish decision and he paid for it with his family.

Lot pitched his tent near Sodom. The cities on the plain, Sodom and Gomorrah, were morally depraved cities. Lot should have had sense enough to stay away from them, but he chose foolishly. Now, Lot didn't move right into Sodom. At first, he just camped nearby, but he camped with the tent facing the city. He wasn't right in it, but he didn't turn his back either. Ask yourself the question: What is your tent pitched toward? You may say to yourself, "I would not go there. I would not do that." But you are sitting on the outskirts, watching it. Once you start moving towards sin, you will eventually end up within its city limits.

4. **What are modern moral equivalents to "pitching our tents toward Sodom"—decisions that can take us one step closer to temptation?**

Here is the first rule of making a defining moment decision. We need to downplay the upside while playing up the downside. Think about everything you do and project yourself into the future. Ask yourself, "Will I be glad I did this when I am 80 years old? Does this really matter? Is it leading me in the direction I really want to go?"

5. **What defining moment decisions are you currently facing?**

God Encounters

Read Genesis 13:18

How do we make wise choices? None of us wants to make dumb moves like Lot. Instead, we want to be people of faith like Abraham—people whom God blesses. One of the outstanding characteristics of Abraham's life was: Every time he had to make a big decision, or had a significant event in his life, he built an altar. An altar, in the Bible, symbolized a close, personal connection with God. It commemorated notable encounters with Him. It was a physical expression of a person's faith. We have that same opportunity to connect with God. We can open our hearts and submit to God, like Abraham did. The way we do that is by praying during, before, and even after we make defining moment decisions. When we pray, we are demonstrating our faith in a God who has a plan for us and who is worthy of being followed.

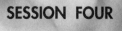

We also need to build around ourselves a board of personal directors. There is wisdom in a number of counselors, people who love us and who will speak truth into our lives. These counselors will be able to say, "You're not thinking clearly about this issue. If you move in this direction, you are heading for disaster. Please stop and think this through." In the midst of a defining moment, if we pull away from people who love us, we are going to make dumb decisions. We need the check and balance of godly, Christ-centered friends.

6. **Who do you have around you who can serve on your personal board of directors? What qualities do they exhibit that make them good advisors?**

Rescued from the Fire

After Lot had lived close to Sodom and Gomorrah for a while, some angels showed up with a message for Abraham from God. God told Abraham that He was going to destroy Sodom and Gomorrah for their sins. He promised Abraham that if 10 righteous men could be found in the city, He would spare it. Although God was ready to wipe out the city, He also provided a way out for them. That is His way. Remember, He destroyed the earth's population in Noah's time, but He saved Noah and his family.

God still provides a way out of destruction for us today. If we got what we deserved, we would be wiped out too, but God provided a way out of our sins. He sent Jesus Christ as a sin sacrifice. He died for our sins and rose again, and if we meet Christ and receive Him, He is our way out.

Read Genesis 19:1-29

At first, Lot only moved *toward* Sodom. But now, Lot was living right *in* Sodom. He may even have been a leader in Sodom because he was sitting in the city gateway, where the elders gathered to handle governmental business. Lot was not only in Sodom; *Sodom was now in Lot.* He moved from being an observer to being part of the sinful system.

This passage portrays the rampant immorality, sexual perversion, and violence of the people of Sodom. We all have different temptations and weaknesses, but each of us is responsible to make our choices according to God's ways. We can never excuse our behavior by saying, "I couldn't help it. That's just the way I am, so I had no choice." Often when we are messing around with sin, we say, "God, I'll just slowly move away from this. I'll just cut back a little at a time, and then I'll finally quit for good." No, you can't. Make a fast break. Some of us right now may be involved in relationships that are messing us up. We may be saying, "Well, I don't want to hurt his feelings." We may be involved in something questionable and we think, "I don't want to make a big deal out of it." Who are you trying to fool? When you realize that you are moving into the suburbs of Sodom, don't think you can slowly drift back out. Make a fast break; run as far away as you can.

Lot hesitated—even though he had just seen first hand the level of wickedness in Sodom—he still hesitated to leave. But God was merciful to him, and the angels just dragged Lot and his family away.

7. **Has God ever rescued you from your own folly? How did He do it?**

8. **Why did God tell Lot and his family not to look back? Why did Lot's wife disobey? What might "looking back" look like in our lives today?**

LIFT IT UP

Decisions come at us rapidly. Trying to discern which decisions are really important overwhelms us. We either pray about what necktie to wear or ignore God altogether. But there is good news. We don't have to grope around in the fog. The Bible supplies clarity about God's thinking on moral issues. When we faithfully keep communication lines open, and work at living to honor God, our defining moment decisions will be made according to God's Word and directed by His Spirit at work in us.

9. **How are your communication lines with God? Do you have a consistent prayer time? Do you ask Him for His input in all your decisions?**

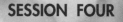

10. **If you feel that you have already made a bad decision in a
    defining moment, remember that it's not too late to repent
    and turn away from Sodom. Lot could have faced his tent
    the opposite direction at any time. How can this group pray
    for and encourage you in defining moments or struggles
    in your life?**

Take time to pray together about defining moment crises or temptations that group members are
currently facing.

My Prayer Needs:

_____

_____

_____

_____

_____

_____

My Group's Prayer Needs:

_____

_____

_____

_____

_____

_____

_____

_____

_____

_____

_____

_____

DEVOTIONALS

DAY 1: **The One Thing**

One thing I ask of the LORD, this is what I seek: that I may dwell in the house of the LORD all the days of my life, to gaze upon the beauty of the LORD and to seek him in his temple (Psalm 27:4).

If you were going to ask just one thing of God, what would it be? Be honest with yourself—what is really the first thing that pops into your mind? Financial success? Healing for a loved one? The solution to a problem in your life? Justification before people who have misjudged you? Sometimes the issues in this world can completely occupy our thoughts. But read again what King David asked for. He wasn't looking for anything connected to life on this earth. He was looking ahead to eternity, and saying, "Nothing else matters. All I want is to be with You."

Write down three of the top things that tend to occupy your mind. How do they compare to spending eternity with Jesus Christ?

DAY 2: **Sneak Peeks of Heaven**

I am still confident of this: I will see the goodness of the LORD in the land of the living. Wait for the LORD; be strong and take heart and wait for the LORD (Psalm 27:13-14).

David's heart was set on eternity, but he wasn't so set on heaven that he was no earthly good. He knew God had experiences for him here on earth. God wants us to trust Him, but He also loves to give us peeks at what heaven will be like. If we wait for His timing, and trust in Him, we are not resigning ourselves to a life of discouragement and dryness, waiting for some "pie in the sky" future. Instead, we are signing up for some incredible experiences, where we will see God's goodness first hand.

Write down as several events that have showed you God's goodness.

DAY 3: **From "Up" to "Down"**

Then the peoples around them set out to discourage the people of Judah and make them afraid to go on building (Ezra 4:4).

Initially, the chance to rebuild the temple seemed incredible! The people had endured 70 years of exile and many deeply repented and turned back to God. Now as they finally return home, they find a bunch of hostile neighbors. Those who remembered the glory of Solomon's temple wept when they saw the small foundation of its replacement. Enthusiasm turned to discouragement, especially as they saw the insignificance of their efforts. Discouragement led to fear and ineffectiveness.

Who or what is your opposition in the hard times of life, when things don't turn out as you expected? Ask God for the insight and power to overcome discouragement.

_____

_____

_____

DAY 4: **Is God Missing This?**

And my God will meet all your needs according to his glorious riches in Christ Jesus (Philippians 4:19).

The hardest thing about hard times is feeling that God is far away. During some crises, we are filled with a strong sense of God's presence and love. When this occurs, hard times can be our best times because of the intimacy we experience with God. During other struggles, we become overwhelmed, or feel abandoned, and it seems there's an impassable wall between us and God. But when we feel spiritually dried up, we can take courage in knowing that God's resources never dry up. Even if we don't "feel" Him, He never forgets us, nor does He neglect any of our needs.

When have you seen God come through for you in a tough time recently? What needs do you feel you have right now? Ask God to fulfill these needs from His storehouse of glorious riches.

_____

_____

_____

DEVOTIONALS

DAY 5: **A Vital Secret**

I know what it is to be in need, and I know what it is to have plenty. I have learned the secret of being content in any and every situation, whether well fed or hungry, whether living in plenty or in want (Philippians 4:12).

When Paul wrote about rejoicing in the Lord, he wasn't typing out trite "truisms" from a padded chair in a high-powered corner office. He was writing from nitty-gritty real life experience. When Paul talked about being at the top, he knew what he was saying. He had been born into a well-to-do family, educated by the best teachers, and considered one of the most promising and brilliant Jewish theologians of his time. He was part of the "in crowd" with a reputation for zealous adherence to the law. He also knew about being on the bottom. He had been beaten, stoned, chased out of town, and tossed in prison several times. He had worked hard to earn his own living while working more than full time as a missionary and church planter. Whatever happened though, he knew the God he served, and that nothing could change the nature of God or the reality of the eternity Paul looked forward to.

What part of your life do you have the hardest time accepting? What would it take to make you truly content?

_____

_____

_____

_____

_____

_____

_____

_____

_____

_____

_____

_____

_____

_____

_____

DEVOTIONALS

DAY 6: **Our Reason for Joy**

Rejoice in the Lord always. I will say it again: Rejoice! (Philippians 4:4).

Always? Surely Paul didn't really mean always. What about when you find out you have cancer? Or, when you lose your job? When you are rejected, or someone you care about dies? You know, those times when God feels so far away! How can we rejoice then? It would be absolute hypocrisy to sing and dance and say, "Hooray! I am miserable! Let's have a party!" But notice that this verse doesn't say, "Pretend everything is okay." It says, "Rejoice in the Lord." No matter what happens, no matter how bad things seem, God is always the same. He is always good and always loving, and we can rejoice that He will continue to care for us and walk through our bad days with us. When we are dealing with dry, desert times in our lives we must learn to say, "God, I don't understand this, and I don't like it, but I know who You are and I know that You are going to turn this into something good. I thank you for working in my life, and turning me into the person You intend for me to be."

What is one aspect of God's character you can be thankful for no matter what else is happening? How does this help you to make it through the tough times?

_____

_____

_____

_____

_____

_____

_____

_____

_____

_____

_____

_____

_____

_____

DEVOTIONALS

DAY 7: **Tough Times and Second Chances**

Anyone of his people among you—may his God be with him, and let him go up to Jerusalem in Judah and build the temple of the LORD, the God of Israel, the God who is in Jerusalem (Ezra 1:3-4).

God had warned Israel in the beginning that if they did not obey Him, they would be punished. Although God was merciful to them again and again, He finally fulfilled His warning, and allowed His people to be taken captive into Babylon. Their exile lasted 70 years as God had promised, and then God worked through Cyrus, the king of Persia, to allow some of the people to return home and begin rebuilding the temple of the Lord.

The people of Israel were going down the drain fast, but that's why God jolted them back through the 70-year captivity. When given the opportunity to go back and start again, the people were excited and jumped at the chance to get on the right track.

When has God given you a second chance to follow Him? How did you respond? Thank God that He takes you through tough times to get you on the right track again.

DEVOTIONALS

DAY 8: **Get With God's Program**

This is what the LORD Almighty says: "These people say, 'The time has not yet come for the LORD's house to be built.'" Then the word of the LORD came through the prophet Haggai: "Is it a time for you yourselves to be living in your paneled houses, while this house remains a ruin?" (Haggai 1:2-3).

Sometimes, when we experience spiritual dryness, it's because we are not being fully obedient to God. The people had started out obeying the Lord with enthusiasm. They knew what He wanted them to do, and they were willing to tackle it. But when things didn't go as expected, they gave up. We often make this same mistake. We look on the tasks God gives us in terms of what we will get. We focus on the temple we are building, rather than on the simple act of obedience. We give up too easily without ever stopping to find out what God wants. Just because we don't see how difficulties fit into the finished picture doesn't mean that God doesn't have an incredible plan.

Write down two things that might, for you, come under the category of "living in your paneled house" instead of doing God's work. Ask God to light a fire under you to give you a passion to obey Him.

_____

_____

_____

_____

_____

_____

_____

_____

_____

_____

_____

_____

_____

DEVOTIONALS

DAY 9: **Less Than Amazing**

"Who of you is left who saw this house in its former glory? How does it look to you now? Does it not seem as nothing? ... The glory of this present house will be greater than the glory of the former house," says the LORD Almighty (Haggai 2:3,9).

The returned exiles were disappointed in the quality of the rebuilt temple. To those who remembered the former temple, this new version must have felt like replacing a beautiful historic mansion with a doublewide mobile home. The workmanship, size, and decorations were all inferior. It was so disappointing to the people that all their work on the temple ground to a halt for a time. What they forgot was that this temple was God's project, not theirs. Even though it was not as glorious as the old building, God would be pleased if they were putting their best efforts into it. As always, God is more interested in obedient hearts than in the amount of gold trimming. Besides, He had amazing future plans for this less-than-amazing temple.

When you feel discouraged about the success of your efforts for God, He doesn't expect you to cheer yourself up. He wants you to ask Him for encouragement. In what areas do you feel the need for encouragement right now?

_____

_____

_____

_____

_____

_____

_____

_____

_____

_____

_____

_____

_____

DEVOTIONALS

DAY 10: **Worth the Wait**

Be patient, then, brothers, until the Lord's coming. See how the farmer waits for the land to yield its valuable crop and how patient he is for the autumn and spring rains. You too, be patient and stand firm, because the Lord's coming is near (James 5:7-8).

We constantly have trouble with timing. We want everything to happen immediately, pronto, now! We're just like little kids planting a first garden. We put seeds in the ground and then go out every day and dig them up so we can see if they are sprouting yet.

When you believed that you have obeyed the Lord and yet things are not turning out as you expected, then there are two things you need to do. First, make sure you really did what God wanted. Sometimes, you look back and see that your motives were selfish, or that you did something clearly against God's direction in Scripture. If your disappointment is due to disobedience, you must repent and go God's way. Second, if you are sure that you acted the best way you knew, and are not in sin, you must simply wait. Seeds take a long time to grow, and God's timetable is different than ours.

What "crops" are you waiting to see grow right now? Ask God to give you a long-term perspective and trust in Him so that you can wait for His timing.

_____

_____

_____

_____

_____

_____

_____

_____

_____

_____

_____

_____

_____

_____

Dry as a Bone ...
Growing in Life's Deserts (Moses)

Exodus 2:11-25, 3:1-14, 4:10-16

God has created us in His image and given us a great capacity for experience. The desire and capacity to experience God's presence is God-given as well. But we don't experience spiritual "highs" 24/7. Most of us experience times when we feel God is far away. We've got to know that God is working even in the "desert times." He can use every experience to teach us and prepare us for what is ahead.

START IT UP

Even if you think you've led a dull life, each person has had unique experiences. Your unique experiences have formed you.

1. **Who is one of the most interesting people you have met?**

2. **What is an experience you have had that you think is unique to your group?**

TALK IT UP

Many of us long for real, personal experiences with God. We need a spark to ignite us. In this session, we will discuss some events in the life of Moses—a man who truly experienced God.

Stuck in the Desert

Read Exodus 2:11-25

Moses was born into Egyptian slavery in a time when it was tough to be alive. The Pharaoh of Egypt wanted to curb the Hebrew baby boom, so he asked the midwives to kill all the male babies as they were born. Of course, the midwives and the mothers worked together to protect these children and one of them was saved in a miraculous way. The Hebrew baby, Moses, was adopted by Pharaoh's daughter. He was raised as part of the "first family" of a powerful nation. He was educated in the best schools, he was wealthy, and he was part of the "in crowd." He was as far removed from his beginnings as a slave as you could imagine.

When he was 40 years old, he walked outside and saw an Egyptian abusing a Hebrew slave. Now Moses had not been brought up to think of himself as a Hebrew, but when he saw this happen, his blood boiled. He looked at the Egyptian, and thought, "That guy is destroying one of my brothers!" (From that time on, Moses identified himself as a Hebrew.) In a flash, he reached out and killed the Egyptian. Moses thought no one had seen this dirty deed, but word leaked out in the Hebrew community. Moses grew scared and fled. He was afraid of what would happen when Pharaoh found out. But more importantly, he suddenly realized he was not Egyptian and yet he had no place with his own people either. He was in the desert for many years and felt like an "alien" there.

3.   **What kinds of experiences do you think could be metaphorically described as spiritual deserts?**

What Moses didn't realize was that God was working out a plan for his life. God had miraculously saved that little baby and arranged for his education in the best schools at Pharaoh's expense for a reason. Everything that happened to Moses was part of God's preparation for what Moses would become and these years in the Egyptian desert were no exception.

4.   **As you look back over your life, what are some experiences that God used to prepare you for what was ahead?**

SESSION FIVE

A Dry and Desolate Place

Read Exodus 3:1-14

The Bible doesn't spend much time talking about Moses' time in the desert. The narrative skips from the time he ran away to the time when God revealed his destiny. But somewhere in the narrative a little piece of information is mentioned: Moses was in the desert for a "long period"—likely around forty years.

The desert is a dry and desolate place. It's also a place where you're alone. We all go through times that make us feel we are alone in a spiritual desert. Maybe you received a bad report from the doctor and you're in a health desert. It could be a marital desert or a child-rearing desert. Maybe it's an emotional desert. God allows desert times for a reason. When we are alone in a desert, we are finally ready to listen to God.

5. How do you react when you face a "desert" time in your life?

Usually we complain. We say, "God, I don't deserve this! I don't need this." We think that we are too spiritual or too strong for desert dwelling. We get impatient, "Well, okay, I'll just learn a quick lesson and then I need to get back to my agenda. I have things to do."

Scripture doesn't tell us how Moses reacted to his desert dwelling, but when God came to reveal His plan for Moses' future, Moses didn't respond with resentment or anger. He was humble and, ultimately, obedient.

When we come to the point where we can finally say, "Lord, have your way in my life. I know your desert is the best for me" ... we can change. Then we're ready to hear what God wants to say to us. God pursues an intimate and authentic love relationship with us and He allows desert times in our lives so we can hear Him speaking to us in our aloneness and struggles.

6. What good have you seen come out of a "desert" experience in your life?

God Seeks Us Out

God pursues a deep and intimate relationship with us. Often you hear people say, "I found the Lord," but in reality, it is God who finds us. He is out looking for us, calling us to come to Him. If we ever understand what it means to experience God on a day to day basis, we must first learn that God is a pursuing God. He is the One who pursues a relationship with us—whether we want it or not.

Too often we ignore Him. He beats on the door of our lives and we don't answer because we fear He will require us to change. We need to respond to His pursuit by saying, "I know You're seeking me and that You're going to change me for the better." That is where our trek out of the desert begins.

7. What is the area of your life that is hardest to give to God?

A Peek at God's Plans

God not only seeks us out, He also gives us a peek into what He plans to do with us. God has to get our attention before He can speak to us. God speaks through people and events. He speaks through songs and experiences. He speaks into our hearts and most obviously through His Book. He even spoke to Moses through a burning bush! God is a God who desires to communicate with us. But often we miss God's words because we are so caught up in our own plans. One of the best prayers we can pray is simply: "God, help me to recognize when you are speaking to me."

8. What has God used to get your attention recently? How has God communicated with you?

The difficulty is that we're not locked into God and we miss Him communicating through ordinary events. And because we miss him through the ordinary, we don't live extraordinary lives. Then we feel dry spiritually because we are missing God.

What is God showing you about your marriage? What is He showing you about your career? What is He showing you about how to nurture your children? God is trying to get your attention Then He's going to say, "Okay, here's what I'm planning for you." But first we have to learn to listen.

God Uses the Weak

God seeks us and gives us a peek at His plans for us. We may not feel important enough for God to make plans for but He specializes in using the weak.

Read Exodus 4:10-16

When Moses saw God and heard His plans, Moses' immediate response was not, "Great, you really picked the right guy for this job. I'll go out and win." His response was essentially, "I'm weak. I can't do that!" And, like Moses, we too are weak. We're sinners, all of us. But it's not about us—it's about Who is working through us.

God's response to the weak isn't just "I understand you're not up to the task; don't worry about it." No, He uses weak people all the time. But He also has plans to mold us into better shape to fit the plans He has for us. If we are willing to make some adjustments in our lives, we can become the kind of people God envisions us to become. How can you make these major adjustments in your marriage, your career, your ministry, or your parenting unless you know what God wants for your life? We must be willing to make adjustments. But first we must be in communication with God so that we are sure of what He's saying to us.

9. **Why was God angry with Moses? Has God ever asked you to do something that you really didn't want to do? What happened?**

LIFT IT UP

Moses could have chosen to stay in the desert forever. He could have said, "No way God, I'm not moving out of my comfort zone and I'm not planning to change either." Getting out of the desert requires submission to God and it might be painful. But obedience enables us to experience God in an incredible way.

Believe that God wants to speak to you. He wants you to experience Him and interact on a daily basis. We need to say, "God, I'm glad I'm in your hands. I'm just this blob of clay. Mold me. Make me. Shape me." It's not always fun to be clay. But God can make something beautiful out of our lives if we allow Him to take charge fully. And again, we need to say, "God, I am a sinner. I am weak. I am frail. I can't do it. I've got to rely on an infusion of your grace and mercy and power. God, help me to realize You are with me in this desert time."

10. **What are the deserts in your life right now? What do you think God is trying to say to you now whether or not you are in a desert time?**

11. **Have you thanked God for the desert times in your life? They don't seem fun, but God is working on us to make us into His kind of people. What specific changes or outcomes can you thank Him for?**

Take time to pray together about the deserts each one is traveling just now. Make a commitment to travel together, encouraging each other in your journeys.

My Prayer Needs:

_____

_____

_____

My Group's Prayer Needs:

_____

_____

_____

_____

_____

_____

_____

_____

_____

_____

_____

_____

_____

DEVOTIONALS

DAY 1: **Is God Really Safe?**

All the ways of the LORD are loving and faithful for those who keep the demands of his covenant (Psalm 25:10).

Many times, we struggle with following God's lead because we're just not sure that He is really trustworthy. We think, "What if He lets me down? What if I do this and then everything turns out badly?" We are afraid of taking our own hands off the steering wheel and letting God navigate for us. After all, sometimes God does things that hurt or are uncomfortable. When we think this way, it is because we have lost track of Who God is. Sure, sometimes His ways hurt. Sometimes we don't like what He does. But God is not just playing around with us. Everything He does is for a purpose, and it is based on His love and faithfulness.

How has God shown love or faithfulness to you recently? What fears or concerns do you have about handing Him the steering wheel of your life? Discuss these with Him in prayer.

DAY 2: **Real Life is Upside Down**

Then Jesus said to his disciples, "If anyone would come after me, he must deny himself and take up his cross and follow me. For whoever wants to save his life will lose it, but whoever loses his life for me will find it (Matthew 16:24-25).

Jesus went right to the heart of our issue in following as He talked to His disciples. The reason we struggle to follow God's lead is because we are still basically self-centered. We want to have our own way, do our own thing, and protect our own skins. This seems both safe and natural, but Jesus told us that we have it upside down. In God's kingdom, the ones willing to give up their own agendas and follow Him completely, even if it means losing their lives, are going to win in the end.

What things do you find it hardest to deny yourself? What part of your life are you struggling to yield fully to God?

DEVOTIONALS

DAY 3: **Human Bondage**

Don't you know that when you offer yourselves to someone to obey him as slaves, you are slaves to whom you obey— whether you are slaves to sin, which leads to death, or to obedience, which leads to righteousness? (Romans 6:16).

We talk a lot about personal freedom. We hear about freedom to control our own bodies, finances, or relationships. In reality, we are not free. Whatever we give ourselves to will become our master. We only get to decide which master we will serve. We can submit ourselves to God, and be made more and more like Him, or we can submit to our sinful desires, and become slaves to sin. There is no way to get around it. We may think that by avoiding God's requirements we is free, but in reality we have only chosen a different master—one who hates us and wants to drive us to despair and ruin.

Look back over the things you have done this week. Given your actions, who would you say was you master? In what areas are you still a slave to sin?

_____

_____

_____

DAY 4: **No Place to Hide**

So then, each of us will give an account of himself to God (Romans 14:12).

It's impossible to hide from God. If He has asked us to do something we don't want to do, our human response is to try to hide from Him. We act like babies who think they are hidden when they cover their eyes. "If I can't see you, you can't see me." When God calls us to follow Him, we have exactly one wise choice: obedience. We can't refuse to do what He wants, and then hope He'll forget, or not notice, or change His mind. In the end, we will all have to stand before Him and answer for our lives.

What would you really rather not have to stand before God and answer for? Read 1 John 1:9. The amazing news is that He has promised to forgive our sins when we humbly confess and turn from our sinful choices Take time now to confess and make the turn.

_____

_____

_____

DEVOTIONALS

DAY 5: **Close Friends With Jesus**

You are my friends if you do what I command. I no longer call you servants, because a servant does not know his master's business. Instead, I have called you friends, for everything that I learned from my Father I have made known to you (John 15:14-15).

It is true that the guiding force we choose will drive us, whether it is God who teaches us righteousness, or Satan who tempts us to follow our own sin and end up in bondage. But God does not want our service as mindless puppets, or as slaves coerced against our wills. God bought and paid for us with His own blood, but it was in order to adopt us as His sons and daughters, to bring us into a relationship with Him as His friends. Love for God equals obedience, but it is not obedience to a tyrant who expects mindless compliance. It is the obedience of a secure child to a loving father, or a well-loved friend to a beloved mentor. God has made obedience easy for us by telling us what it is for: He is working to form us into beautiful and perfect reflections of His own goodness and love.

What is the hardest thing God has ever asked you to do? How do you think it has helped you look more like Him?

DEVOTIONALS

DAY 6: **Straightened Brains**

Trust in the LORD with all your heart and lean not on your own understanding; in all your ways acknowledge him, and he will make your paths straight (Proverbs 3:5-6).

You may not have noticed this, but humans don't always reason very clearly. We like to think of ourselves as logical, scientific, analytical creatures, capable of figuring things out and running our own lives. Logic and analysis are a part of the amazing mental faculties God has given us, but they are not infallible. Human reasoning is also snarled up with emotions, lack of information, skewed perspective, and sometimes sin and self-deception. The longer we live, the more we realize that we cannot rely on our reasoning to be accurate. Sometimes we will be right; other times we will feel completely correct and be completely wrong. We have only one way out of this dilemma. God is the only One we can trust to untangle wrong thinking. When we trust in Him and ask Him for advice, He will straighten out our minds and show us what He wants us to do.

Write down the dilemma that is troubling you most right now. How much are you relying on your own understanding? Trust in God with all your heart; do what He directs. Write down your prayer and revisit it later to see how God has answered your need.

DEVOTIONALS

DAY 7: **In the Race or On the Couch?**

Do you not know that in a race all the runners run, but only one gets the prize? Run in such a way as to get the prize (1 Corinthians 9:24).

We often drift along in life, avoiding the whole issue of obedience. We seem to think that it won't really matter too much whether we obey God or not. This "couch potato" attitude about life produces ineffective, spiritually flabby Christ-followers. We think that obedience is optional—we can do it if we want extra credit, but it isn't required. Nothing could be farther from the truth. It is just a tiny little step from laziness to outright rebellion against God, and rebellion is something God will not tolerate. If you are drifting instead of obeying, it's time to put on your running shoes and get in the race. Life with Christ may not always be relaxing, but it is guaranteed to keep you awake and to bring many rewards now and in eternity.

Are you in the race for God's prize or are you watching from your couch? In what area of your life is God challenging to get into the race?

DEVOTIONALS

DAY 8: **Backing Up to Go Forward**

I am sending him—who is my very heart—back to you ... no longer as a slave, but better than a slave, as a dear brother. He is very dear to me but even dearer to you, both as a man and as a brother in the Lord (Philemon 12,16).

Paul's letter to Philemon tells the story of the runaway slave, Onesimus, who had come to know Jesus Christ after he escaped. Paul was sending Onesimus back to his master, carrying this letter—a loving request from Paul to Philemon that he set his slave free and treat him as a brother. Onesimus could not know whether Philemon would agree to Paul's request or not. There is little doubt that he had stolen from his master, in addition to running away, so he would have had every reason to expect a beating or worse. It must have been hard to do, but Onesimus had to go back to his master, and make things right with him before he could go on with Christ.

God is a God of love and forgiveness. When we sincerely turn away from our sins and live for Him, He will forgive our sins, and make us clean again. But, God doesn't let us gloss over sins. When we return to Him after wandering off on our own, the first thing He does is take us back to the place where we failed, and give us a chance to make it right.

Is there a place where you have failed to obey God recently? Have you gone back to make things right?

DEVOTIONALS

DAY 9: **How Does Your Garden Grow?**

The one who sows to please his sinful nature, from that nature will reap destruction; the one who sows to please the Spirit, from the Spirit will reap eternal life. Let us not become weary in doing good, for at the proper time we will reap a harvest if we do not give up (Galatians 6:8-9).

Life is just like a garden—what we grow depends on what we plant. If we "plant" habits of obedience to God, we will "grow" a character that is more and more like Christ. If we "plant" laziness, rebellion, or arguments against obedience, we will "grow" discontent, unhappiness, unproductiveness, and sin. Planting to please the Holy Spirit is hard work—that kind of gardening requires weeding, cultivating, fertilizing, and more weeding. Planting to please ourselves is a lot easier—in fact, it is just about as easy as planting weeds. There's no need to mow, or fertilize, or cultivate, and by the end of the summer you will reap a fine crop of hay fever, all without sweat or bother. But what do you really want your life to grow? One way we grow death; the other way life!

In what parts of your life are you sowing weed seed? What kind of weeding do you need to do in your life right now? No matter the state of your spiritual garden, don't give up. God promises an awesome harvest.

DEVOTIONALS

DAY 10: **Not Just a Little Smarter**

As the heavens are higher than the earth, so are my [the LORD's] ways higher than your ways and my thoughts than your thoughts (Isaiah 55:9).

As we are learning to follow God's lead, there is one really important thing that we have to remember: God knows universe-loads more than we do. This is not a surprise, but sometimes we act like we don't know it. We read God's Word, and we say, "Well, I am just sure He doesn't really mean that. After all, we live in a different era, an enlightened age. We don't need archaic ideas." We may not actually say it so many words, but we think our own ideas are better than what the Bible provides. In reality, the difference between what we know and understand and what God knows and understand is more than we can even comprehend. God is not just a smarter human; He's completely and totally beyond our realm—like comparing the intelligence of a piece of dust with that of a person. Let's let God be God.

Write down something you are particularly glad to leave in God's hands. What is one thing that you tend to think you can handle yourself? Acknowledge God's inconceivable greatness in your prayer time today.

IGN|TE

Refining and Purifying Your Faith

Fish Bait ...
Following God's Lead (Jonah)

Jonah 1:1-17, 2:1-10, 3:1-5,10, 4:1-11

Do you remember playing "Follow the Leader" as a little child? Everyone would line up and the "leader" would walk, run, do jumping jacks or hop on one leg. Everyone else in the line was supposed to do the same thing. Pretty soon, of course, someone gets tired of following and wants to be the leader. "Hey! It's my turn to be the leader now!"

Isn't that exactly how we act with God? For a while we may be content to follow His lead, but then we decide we don't like how He is leading or we just want to have it our way. We say, "You know, I think it's my turn to decide what to do next." We want to drop God's lead and do our own thing.

START IT UP

As kids, we may take turns leading in the games we play. But as adults, we understand that there is only one Leader who is completely trustworthy: God Himself.

1. **What are some of your favorite games, past and present?**

2. **In general, do you like to organize and direct or would you rather stay in the background? Why is that?**

TALK IT UP

Following God's lead isn't always obvious or easy. But it is always mandatory. In this session, we will examine the life of Jonah, who learned the hard way that God expects complete obedience. From the life of Jonah, we discover some important truths about following God's lead in our lives.

You Can Run, But You Cannot Hide

The first whale-sized principle is that when you run away from God there will be consequences.

Read Jonah 1:1-17

We don't know exactly how the word of the Lord came to Jonah, but Jonah had no doubt Who was speaking to him. Jonah was sure God was talking; he just didn't like God's message.

> **3. Have you ever heard a message that you were pretty sure was from God, but you really didn't like it? How can we tell if a message is from God or not?**

In the Christian life there are only two destinations: Nineveh (obedience), and Tarshish (disobedience). All of us are heading toward one city or the other. You can't straddle them with one foot in obedience and the other in disobedience.

Jonah went down to Joppa and found a ship headed toward disobedience. Satan, the Evil One, will always provide transportation to Tarshish. Just because the circumstances seem right and the ticket is cheap, does not mean it's the will of God. Satan is the ultimate travel agent. If you are having marital troubles, he will provide someone at the office that looks like a better ship. This can happen in every area of life: home, business, family and friends, ministry, and personal life. We are either headed for Nineveh or Tarshish.

The next time you are tempted to say, "Oh, it must be God's will because the circumstances are working out and everything is cool," stop and remember Jonah. He seemed to have the perfect circumstances for his getaway, but that did not mean God was approving and blessing him. Jonah knew exactly what God wanted him to do but chose to disobey. God won't necessarily thwart our getaway plans and force our obedience; He's given us free will.

4. **How can we tell whether or not favorable circumstances are God's blessings?**

Jonah paid his fare and thought he was sneaking away. He thought he'd found a cheap way to escape the hard task God had given him. But Jonah found that disobedience ended up being more costly—and not just for him. Disobedience harms those around us; we can't disobey in a vacuum. When we start a storm, others suffer from it, too. If we choose disobedience, we will always pay —a higher fare than we ever imagined. On the other hand, obedience takes us where we want to go and the Lord will pay the fare.

5. **What high-priced consequences to sin have you seen or experienced?**

The Power of Prayer

Read Jonah 2

Here is a second whale-sized principle: prayer will take you from the pit to the pinnacle. To follow God's lead, we have to pray. Jonah gives us a good example of how to pray. He prayed a tenderhearted confession—a heart that told the truth about his condition. Sin is a blockade to our relationship with God. So we have to confess the truth about our sins to remove the barriers between God and us. Secondly, Jonah prayed Scripture as he poured his heart out to God. But before we can pray Scripture, we need to know enough of the Bible to recall it when we need to resist temptation. Regular time in the God's Word will nourish our attitudes and character so we can obey God in the tough times.

Jonah tried but he couldn't get away from God. He was running, but God was running right beside him. However far you run, you can't get away from God.

6. **What keeps you from wanting to pray when you've been running from God? Are those reasons based on truth or misconceptions about God?**

Second Chances

Read Jonah 3:1-5,10

This is the third whale-sized principle: we have to seize the moment of second chances. Our great God gave Jonah a second chance to obey. The message of second chances runs throughout the Bible. Moses smashed the Ten Commandments when he saw the Israelites sin, but God gave them a second chance. David, a man after God's own heart, was at the peak of his career when he committed adultery and then arranged to have the woman's husband killed. But he repented and God gave him another chance. Samson dabbled in disobedience and lost the gifts God had given him. But God gave Samson a second chance to serve. Simon Peter denied Jesus three times, but Jesus gave him the chance to take it back. Jonah disobeyed, but "then the word of Lord came to Jonah a second time" (Jonah 3:1).

We serve a God of second chances. Maybe God is giving you a second chance today. Maybe you started following Him but gave it up. Perhaps you ignored an opportunity He wanted you to take. Will you accept God's gracious offer of a second chance?

7. **When has God given you a second chance? How did you feel when this occurred?**

Heart Tune-ups

Read Jonah 4:1-11

This brings us to the fourth whale-sized principle. Up to chapter four, Jonah's repentance looks pretty solid. God delivered him; he preached to Nineveh and 120,000 people were saved. Jonah obeyed, but he didn't really want to see Nineveh saved. He was looking forward to seeing it destroyed and he was upset when God didn't do it. Jonah's act of repentance was right, but his heart was not yet in tune with God's heart.

If we are going to follow God's lead, we need to ask God to give us compassion. You see, God cares about all people. Jonah thought that God just cared about the Jews. He couldn't grasp the fact that God cared for those sorry, sinful Ninevites. We often are like Jonah and concern ourselves with a dying vine, when God is interested in perishing people. Jonah was upset because God wasn't working the way Jonah liked. He thought he knew how God thought. We need to learn, as Jonah did, that every time, we try to put God in a box we get into trouble.

8. **Who do you have the hardest time seeing as someone God loves? Why do you think you feel this way? What should you do about it?**

LIFT IT UP

God is continually leading us out of our comfort zones. He asks us to go places we don't want to go, to say things we don't want to say, and to love people we consider unlovable. We may even feel like God is out to get us. He won't quit hounding us and He won't let us stay in the comfort zone. But stop and think about it. Do you really want Him to? Do you want God to leave you alone and let you turn into a spiritual couch potato? Or do you want Him to love you, to communicate with you and build you into a person who is strong, wise, and compassionate? It's your choice!

9. **Have you been running away from something God wants you to do? It's not too late to step off the ship called "Disobedience" and start for Nineveh. Share your struggle with the group so they can pray with you.**

10. Is there something God wants you to do and you want to obey, but you're still scared to move ahead on? Let this group pray with you for encouragement and strength.

Take time to pray together to discern what God might be calling you to do. Share your struggles with obedience and consider setting up some accountability measures with each other.

My Prayer Needs:

_____

_____

_____

_____

_____

_____

My Group's Prayer Needs:

_____

_____

_____

_____

_____

_____

_____

_____

_____

_____

_____

_____

DEVOTIONALS

DAY 1: **Useful or Useless?**

Land that drinks in the rain often falling on it and that produces a crop useful to those for whom it is farmed receives the blessing of God (Hebrews 6:7).

Sometimes we fence-sit even after we make the decision to submit our lives to Christ. We want to sit and soak, and never take the next step of acting out our faith. But if we drink in spiritual teaching without living it out, we are going to become bloated and waterlogged. We won't be any good to anyone. If we will be like the good ground that receives the blessing of God, we have to get up and start stepping out in faith. We have to act as though we really believe what we say we believe.

Write down the first two things that come to mind when you think about living with conviction. Are these things you do? Why do you do them (or not do them)?

_____

_____

_____

DAY 2: **Don't Look Back**

Brothers, I do not consider myself yet to have taken hold of it. But one thing I do: Forgetting what is behind and straining toward what is ahead, I press on toward the goal to win the prize for which God has called me heavenward in Christ Jesus (Philippians 3:13-14).

When we study Paul's life, we see a man of incredible intelligence and abilities, totally sold out for God. And yet, even Paul didn't feel like he had it all together. He knew that he failed, again and again. Part of his strength and success came from the fact that he took God at His word regarding forgiveness. "As far as the east is from the west, so far has he removed our transgressions from us" (Psalm 103:12). When we have confessed and God has forgiven, the issue is over. Brooding over past failures (or being puffed up over past victories) will only take our attention off the goal. If we constantly look over our shoulders as we run, we are going to trip and fall, or slow down to a walk.

What "things behind" do you need to "forget" so you can put your attention on the goal?

_____

_____

_____

DEVOTIONALS

DAY 3: **Don't Harden Your Heart**

So, as the Holy Spirit says: "Today, if you hear his voice, do not harden your hearts as you did in the rebellion, during the time of testing in the desert (Hebrews 3:7-8).

Many people who have heard the truth of the gospel, and who may even claim to be Christ-followers, are really fence-sitters. They are attracted to some things about Jesus, and afraid of others. They reason, "I will believe later. I will follow Christ after I finish having fun, after I make a lot of money, or after I retire." But tomorrow may be too late. When the Israelites heard God's response (through Joshua and Caleb) to their fears, they did not listen. They hardened their hearts, and then it was too late. God permanently prohibited them from entering the promised land because of their unbelief.

Have you gotten down off the fence yet? Or will you miss out on eternity because of unbelief? If you have not yet made this decision, don't put it off any longer. Is any part of you still hanging on that fence?

_____

_____

_____

DAY 4: **Children of the Light**

But you brothers, are not in darkness so that this day [the Day of the Lord] should surprise you like a thief. You are all sons of the light and sons of the day. We do not belong to the night or to the darkness. So then, let us not be like others, who are asleep, but let us be alert and self-controlled (1 Thessalonians 5:4-6).

We have a very good reason to stop fence-sitting, and stiffening up our wavering backbones: time is short, and we don't know when our lives on this earth will end. Jesus has promised that He will return one day, and that it will be at a time when we don't expect Him. Let's not be spiritually asleep in the dark when He gets here. We know He's coming, so let's get ready by walking in the light of His truth.

Write down some things you would like to do to be ready for Christ's return. Then, ask God to shed His light and truth in your life.

_____

_____

_____

DAY 5: **Wavering is a Waste**

As Paul discoursed on righteousness, self-control and the judgment to come, Felix was afraid and said, "That's enough for now! You may leave. When I find it convenient, I will send for you." At the same time, he was hoping that Paul would offer him a bribe, so he sent for him frequently and talked with him (Acts 24:25-26).

Felix is the essential picture of the seeker who won't let himself seek. He had heard of the teachings of Jesus already—his wife was Jewish, and he had apparently heard some of the disciples preach, or at least heard of what they were saying. He must have been familiar enough with his wife's religion to be able to understand a lot about where this new "Way" was coming from. Felix was interested all right—but he was also scared. When Paul started to talk about the difficult parts, Felix wavered. He couldn't make up his mind. He didn't want to give up his own way, but neither did he want to give up hearing about Jesus. Felix continued to waver for two more years, and apparently never did make a decision.

The moral: procrastination will eventually catch up with you. Christ-followers sometimes exhibit the same kind of wavering as Felix. In what area have you been wavering in following and obeying God?

_____

_____

_____

_____

_____

_____

_____

_____

_____

_____

_____

_____

DEVOTIONALS

DAY 6: **God to the Rescue**

But the LORD said to me, "Do not say, 'I am only a child.' You must go to everyone I send you to and say whatever I command you. Do not be afraid of them, for I am with you and will rescue you," declares the LORD (Jeremiah 1:7-8).

Jeremiah was a man who was given a very difficult job. God appointed him to be His prophet to a rebellious people not at all interested in Jeremiah's message. He felt too immature and inexperienced to know how to start, and when he did start, he experienced nothing but rejection from the people he was sent to reach. Jeremiah's life wasn't easy, but he had the best of encouragements to keep on going. It wasn't Jeremiah's job that Jeremiah was doing, it was God's job, and therefore God promised to provide the resources.

God is calling every one of His followers to stand up with the same kind of conviction as Jeremiah. The thought of it can make our knees tremble, and our hearts shrink back. But we must remember that God will be with us, just as He was for Jeremiah.

What person of conviction has inspired you? What particularly stood out to you about this person? Pray for passionate conviction in your life.

DAY 7: **Convicted for Convictions**

Then they called them in again and commanded them not to speak or teach at all in the name of Jesus. But Peter and John replied, "Judge for yourselves whether it is right in God's sight to obey you rather than God. For we cannot help speaking about what we have seen and heard" (Acts 4:18-20).

The religious rulers of the day didn't care whether Peter and John were speaking the truth as they preached about "this Jesus." All they cared about was shutting these two troublemakers up forever, and stopping the spread of the amazing story of the healing of the crippled beggar. So, they did the obvious thing. They arrested Peter and John, and threw them into prison. The next day, these two were brought before the Sanhedrin, the Jewish religious court, and sternly told to drop their teachings about Jesus, or else the religious leaders would make serious trouble for them.

Peter and John undoubtedly knew of the power this group possessed. (After all, this same group had managed to condemn Jesus to death.) But in spite of the threats and intimidation, Peter and John stood firm. Their conviction to the truth was real, and nothing could shake that.

In what kinds of situations today might a person have to take a stand between obeying God and obeying some other authority? Where do you need more conviction in your own life?

_____

_____

_____

_____

_____

_____

_____

_____

_____

_____

_____

_____

_____

DEVOTIONALS

DAY 8: **The Blessing of Rejection**

Blessed are you when men hate you, when they exclude you and insult you and reject your name as evil, because of the Son of Man (Luke 6:22).

Some years ago, in a small town, a young boy eagerly anticipated joining a popular youth organization. The kids involved seemed to have so much fun—they did projects together, went to rallies and parties and talked with enthusiasm about their leaders and their vision for a new and better future. It was obvious that to be "in," you had to be part of this group.

Near the same time, a second exciting event was approaching in this boy's life. It was his turn to serve as an altar boy in his church. Each of his brothers had served before him, and his father and grandfather had taken their turns when they were boys themselves. He looked forward to helping the priest serve the rest of the congregation. Then the blow fell. The leaders of the youth organization informed him that as long he was taking active part in religion, he was out of the club. Period. He felt terribly rejected, but the young men of his family always served as altar boys, and it simply wouldn't do to quit. He dropped out of the youth organization, but it hurt to be left behind when all his friends went off together.

Rejection is painful, and we try to avoid it, but it isn't the worst thing that can happen. To the end of his life, that boy thanked God that he had been kicked out of the Hitler Youth.

When have you felt rejected because of something you believe in? From your perspective now, what good can you see that came out of that event?

_____

_____

_____

_____

_____

_____

_____

_____

_____

_____

_____

DEVOTIONALS

DAY 9: **Out of the "In Group"**

Joshua son of Nun and Caleb son of Jephunneh, who were among those who had explored the land, tore their clothes and said to the entire Israelite assembly, "The land we passed through and explored is exceedingly good. If the Lord is pleased with us, he will lead us into that land, a land flowing with milk and honey, and will give it to us ... But the whole assembly talked about stoning them (Numbers 14:6-8,10).

Joshua and Caleb found out that being willing to stand up for the Lord did not make them popular. They had gone with 10 other men into the land of Canaan, to check out the area and inhabitants. They found clusters of grapes so big it took two men to carry them, fertile fields, fine vineyards, and luscious orchards. The news they brought back about the inhabitants was not as positive. According to 10 of the spies, the inhabitants were giants who could crush Israel with one blow. They had forgotten God's sure promise that He would be the One to drive out the Canaanites.

Joshua and Caleb were not thanked for reminding the people of God's words. They were not welcome prophets. But that didn't change the truth of their message.

Sometimes we hesitate to stand up for the truth because we don't want to face personal rejection. What people or groups do you most want to stay "in" with? Does this group help or hinder you in standing up for God?

DEVOTIONALS

DAY 10: **Our Real Home**

But our citizenship is in heaven. And we eagerly await a Savior from there, the Lord Jesus Christ, who by the power that enables him to bring everything under his control, will transform our lowly bodies so that they will be like his glorious body. Therefore, my brothers, you whom I love and long for, my joy and crown, that is how you should stand firm in the Lord, dear friends! (Philippians 3:20-4:1).

When we stand firm in our convictions, we may well be rejected, ridiculed, or persecuted. We may be labeled nut cases, or worse. After all, Jesus experienced all of this! But in the end, opinions and labels aren't what are going to count. We must learn to think about life from a different angle. Instead of asking, "Is this going to be comfortable or fun?" we need to ask, "How can this help me be more like Jesus?" and "How does a citizen of heaven respond?" We can stand firm, not because it will be easy and pleasant, but because we know that Jesus is coming back, and that when He comes, we will be transformed to be like Him.

Read 1 Thessalonians 5:9-11. Thank God that you will one day live together with Him. As a citizen of heaven, whom could you encourage and build up this week?

Clash of the Titans ...
Embracing Strong Convictions

(Elijah vs. Jezebel and King Ahab)

1 Kings 18:16-45; James 5:17

Convictions are not popular in our society. Our culture claims that truth is relative. The phrase on the lips of many is, "Whatever you believe is fine for you, but don't let it mess with how I live." So we find it easier to keep quiet about our faith. We keep our beliefs about God compartmentalized and don't allow them to spill over into daily life.

In this session we'll discuss a man with strong convictions. His name, Elijah, means "Yahweh is God," and this was the theme of his life. Elijah was a man "on fire" for God, passionate to serve Him. As we look at Elijah's life, we see a life of adventure, which resulted from standing firmly for what he believed. The great news is that we can have this exciting life, too.

START IT UP

Having a strong conviction about something does not make it truth, but it does affect how we behave.

1. **When you were a child, did you really believe in Santa Claus? Did your belief affect your behavior in November and December?**

2. **Who is a person (either in history or in your life) whom you have admired because of his or her strong convictions?**

TALK IT UP

Convictions Shape Conduct

Convictions shape conduct. In other words, what we believe affects how we behave. However, our "politically correct" culture cries, "Make your own way—whatever conviction you hold is right if you're sincere about it. If you think it's true, then it's true for you."

3. **Will this "politically correct" logic lead to order and peace or disorder and chaos? Why do you think so?**

Unfortunately, our culture is not known for its clear thinking. The truth is that any ideology is either true or false. Whether we are convinced or not doesn't determine its truth. You can be strongly convicted of right or wrong but how you feel about truth is not the same as the fact of truth. So how do we know what is really true? We need to find the source of truth—the absolute. Once we find the absolute, then we base our convictions on that truth. That's why Jesus pointed to the source of absolute truth in John 14 when said, "I am the truth."

Once we know Jesus Christ, we know the source of truth and we will have strong convictions based on truth as He defined it. Strong convictions tend to set us afire for God's way—for truth and life.

Some people have strong convictions; they are on fire for God already. But many people who claim to be Christ-followers really have one foot in and one foot out. Sometimes they believe Christ has the truth and they want to follow Him. Other times, they think it looks too hard, or not so attractive, and so they keep one foot in the world.

Read 1 Kings 18:16-45

King Ahab was running the show in Israel. Earlier in his life, he made a disastrous decision to marry a princess named Jezebel. She was heavily involved in Baal worship and she wrapped Ahab around her little finger. The king of Israel, who was supposed to lead the chosen people in worship of the one true God, let Jezebel lead them into worshipping the pagan god, Baal. God's people, who should have marched into the castle and run off both Ahab and Jezebel, were following right along. They set up shrines and altars to sacrifice to Baal and joined in on the worship of sex, lust for money and possessions, and power. At the same time, they tried to keep one foot in God's camp. They didn't get rid of His temple and worship, but they tried to worship both. They wavered back and forth between two opposite convictions.

4. **What are some areas where people today try to waver between opposing convictions?**

Convictions Ignite Conflict

When people try to avoid making decisions regarding their beliefs, they naturally hate the sight of a person with strong convictions. A person with conviction reminds them of the decision they are avoiding. Elijah had already engaged in a previous struggle with Ahab. God was not pleased with what was happening in Israel. He gave Ahab the message through Elijah that for three years there would be no rain on the land. God kept His word and the land slowly dried up. Now at the end of the three years, Elijah was meeting with Ahab again. Ahab responded angrily, blaming and threatening Elijah.

5. **How do you respond when the Holy Spirit reminds you of rebellion in your life? How do you respond to the messengers He sends to confront you?**

If you hold strong convictions and you are passionate for God, you will experience conflict. If you are not experiencing the adventure, excitement, and growth of doing battle, you'd better check your spiritual pulse. Conflict is a good thing—because it's a God thing. The Bible describes the Christian life as a fight, a war, and a race. Sin doesn't just lie down or run away when we bark at it. It has to be fought and destroyed.

6. **How can you tell whether you are experiencing conflict because of godly convictions or just because you are being stubborn and opinionated?**

Convictions Brand a Message on Us

Conviction ignites conflict, but conviction also brands a message on us. We would be surprised at how many people are watching our lives to see if we really stick to our convictions.

People want to see strong convictions. They want to see people who are "on fire" for God and possess joy and abundant life. They know their own lives are not working. What they are chasing after is not giving them answers. We claim that following Christ does give us answers. Everyone else is looking at us to see whether it's true. Do we really have conviction? Does it change the way we live? Do the people watching you see Jesus in your life? Do they see you get up and try again when you fall down? Consider what kind of message are you sending with your life.

7. **What character quality do you particularly admire in the godly people you know? How can you work on developing or strengthening this quality in your own life?**

Convictions Spark Decisions

Elijah was dealing with an unstable bunch of people. They weren't concerned with the truth—they just wanted to be left alone. But God isn't interested in "sort of" followers. He is a jealous God who wants all or nothing from us. If you are not giving all of your life and devotion to Him—if your heart is divided—then you are not truly worshiping God.

We may look at this story and say, "Come on, we don't worship Baal nowadays. We can't relate to this idol stuff." Oh, really? Baal worship was based on three things: sex, money, and power. Are you saying these are out of date, that people don't worship them anymore?

The prophets of Baal danced, shouted, and turned themselves inside out for an answer from their god—and got nothing. People today do the same thing. We're asking our gods to answer us. "Hey, sex, answer me! Hey pleasure, answer me! Come on and make me feel fulfilled and satisfied. Possessions, the corner office, the next trip, that'll do it." We are like the prophets of Baal, making fools of ourselves to get the attention of our gods and getting no answer.

8. **What things could become idols in your life? Remember, an idol is simply something that takes your attention and devotion away from God.**

Elijah didn't try to reconcile Baal worship with following the Lord. He didn't buy into the "politically correct" thinking of his day. He came right out and essentially said, "Either God is true, or He isn't. You can't worship God and Baal." Today, our culture claims that all religions are equally true, that "many paths lead to heaven." And yet these religions teach opposite things about who God is. How can they all be true?

You do Satan a favor when you waver. Notice that Elijah didn't give reasons why the people should follow the Lord. He didn't claim that it would solve all their problems. He just challenged people to follow God because He is God. We can't base our decision to follow God on whether we like Him and His ways. Sometimes His way will hurt and we will lose things we want to keep. We don't follow God because we like His way best. We follow Him because He is true, whether we like it or not.

Stop for a minute and think about the sign that God chose to send them. The people didn't want fire. Remember they had been in a drought for three and a half years. They wanted rain. But if God had sent rain, it wouldn't have convinced them, would it? They could have explained it away. In the natural scheme of things, rain falls from heaven regularly. But fire? Now that is something else.

LIFT IT UP

Read James 5:17

Why in the world would James say that Elijah is a man just like one of us? Because it's true! Elijah wasn't an alien or Superman with special powers. He was an ordinary man, but a man who was "on fire" for God. One man or woman, passionately pursuing God, can accomplish anything that God directs and empowers.

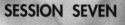

Elijah had only one thing to offer God and it is the same thing we have to offer—a willing heart. But we can't make it on our own. We can't say, "I'm going to have the discipline and courage to carry out my convictions on my own." Instead, we have to say, "God, here I am with my sin and junk. Engulf me by the power and the fire of your Holy Spirit." When we are consumed by Him and our convictions are based in Him, we can stand up before all the armies of darkness. Just one man, because he was on God's team, took out 450 false prophets.

9. What blessings have you experienced in the past through a willingness to obey God?

10. Are you ready to say, "Whatever you want, God," and stand up for His truth? What convictions are you trying to live out? What barriers are standing in your way that this group can help you pull down?

Take time to pray together for strength and endurance.

My Prayer Needs:

_____

_____

_____

My Group's Prayer Needs:

_____

_____

_____

_____

_____

_____

_____

_____

DEVOTIONALS

DAY 1: **Our Great Commission**

Therefore go and make disciples of all nations, baptizing them in the name of the Father and of the Son and of the Holy Spirit, and teaching them to obey everything I have commanded you. And surely I am with you always, to the very end of the age (Matthew 28:19-20).

Once you have yielded your life to Christ, then what? Jesus gave the answer to His disciples just before He returned to heaven—an answer that applies to us, too. The biggest job we have as Christ-followers is to share the good news with others, and then to equip them to live for Christ. Sometimes we forget that spreading the truth about Jesus is really a life or death matter. It isn't just an optional exercise for super-saints. It is something that even the most inarticulate and untrained person can do. If you know what Christ did for you, you know enough to tell someone else the same good news that has changed your life.

Who first told you about Jesus, or helped you to understand who He is and what He has done? Who have you told? Who do you need to tell soon?

DEVOTIONALS

DAY 2: **Preach With Your Life!**

How, then, can they call on the one they have not believed in? And how can they believe in the one of whom they have not heard? And how can they hear without someone preaching to them? (Romans 10:14).

Most of us, when we think of preaching, have one picture in mind: a guy with a microphone standing in front of a crowd, doing all the talking. This is definitely part of what preaching means, and some of us may be called to that kind of ministry. But that isn't even close to the whole picture. We all need to tell people who Jesus is with words—otherwise, how can they believe? But we have to also preach with the way we live our lives. If we say, "Jesus can change your heart," and those around us say, "Well, that sounds very nice, but I happen to live next door to you and I hear you yell at your spouse every day. I work in the same office you do, and I happen to know that you were part of some shady business deals. I play sports with you, and I have heard the kind of jokes you tell" … what kind of message are we really sending?

Do you think your lifestyle is an asset or liability to God's cause? What "wordless preaching" has most affected you? How can you share Jesus in the natural course of life?

_____

_____

_____

_____

_____

_____

_____

_____

_____

_____

_____

_____

_____

_____

DEVOTIONALS

DAY 3: **Power in the Ordinary**

Brothers, think of what you were when you were called. Not many of you were wise by human standards; not many were influential; not many were of noble birth. But God chose the foolish things of the world to shame the wise; God chose the weak things of the world to shame the strong (1 Corinthians 1:26).

We may feel very inadequate to speak out and tell others about Jesus. Many of us fear that we will "turn people off" by not saying just the right thing. Most of all, even if we don't admit it, we fear personal rejection. We think that evangelism would be best left with the wise, intelligent, brave, and saintly few—the ones everyone will listen to because they are important and have charisma. It is true that God does use such people, and they can have an incredible influence. But He also uses plain, ordinary, you and me. Do you realize that most of the world is pretty ordinary? Guess which people are most likely to be able to reach these plain, ordinary people with the truth of Jesus Christ? It's the plain, ordinary ones, who have the same life and struggles. The ones who can say, "I know. I have dealt with that kind of thing, too. This is how Jesus helped me."

Think of two or three people you see regularly who don't know Jesus. Start praying now for the Lord to show you how to connect with these people.

_____

_____

_____

_____

_____

_____

_____

_____

_____

_____

_____

_____

_____

DEVOTIONALS

DAY 4: **Know Your Audience**

Jesus answered, "I tell you the truth, no one can enter the kingdom of God unless he is born of water and the Spirit. Flesh gives birth to flesh, but the Spirit gives birth to spirit. You should not be surprised at my saying, "You must be born again" (John 3:5).

As you read through the Gospels (Matthew, Mark, Luke, and John), you will see that Jesus didn't use just one formula to reach all people. Instead, He tailored His methods according to His audience. He had the wisdom to know just what each individual needed most to hear.

Nicodemus was a member of the Jewish ruling council. He was a man who had studied the Old Testament law from childhood, who desired to live a righteous life, and who was doing all he knew to follow God's requirements. He was curious about Jesus' teaching, but he was afraid of being criticized, so he came by night to find out just what Jesus was up to. Jesus knew exactly what kind of background Nicodemus had. When he began asking questions, Jesus did not hesitate to dive right into a complex theological discussion. Nicodemus knew the law inside out; he had the background to grapple with serious theological matters. He needed the "how," not just the "what." Jesus would not have used this approach with an uneducated person on the streets.

What has been your approach to telling others about Jesus? Look back at your list of people from yesterday. Pray for wisdom about what approach to use with each individual.

_____

_____

_____

_____

_____

_____

_____

_____

_____

_____

DEVOTIONALS

DAY 5: **Straight to the Heart**

Come, see a man who told me everything I ever did. Could this be the Christ? (John 4:29).

For Jesus, as a Jew, to be walking through Samaritan territory was unheard of given the historic animosity between these two groups. His talking to the solitary woman at the well was even more unusual. Jesus knew exactly what kind of person she was—the very fact that she was at the well in the middle of the day showed that she was some kind of societal outcast. Nevertheless, He treated her as a friend and an equal, asking her for a drink. He didn't beat around the bush with small talk, but immediately turned the conversation to spiritual matters. The woman tried to deflect the focus away from her spiritual need by starting an argument over doctrine and religious practice, but Jesus didn't get sidetracked. He knew her problems were not philosophical, and He aimed straight for the heart as He lovingly confronted her sins and need for a Savior.

As a result of Jesus' loving concern and insight, the woman not only believed that Jesus was the promised Savior from God, but she also ran immediately to tell of her discovery to the rest of the village—the same people who had undoubtedly treated her as an outcast.

Of all the people you know, who seems like the most unlikely candidate for becoming a follower of Christ? Start praying for this person now and ask God to open his or her heart to the truth. What can you do to reach out to this person?

_____

_____

_____

_____

_____

_____

_____

_____

_____

_____

_____

_____

DEVOTIONALS

DAY 6: **Signs and Wonders**

Then the man said, "Lord, I believe," and he worshipped him (John 9:38).

Miracles are so awe-inspiring that it seems to us that anyone who saw a miracle would be bound to become an instant believer in Christ. The fact is, miracles don't always affect people that way. Some people seem to be able to reason and twist anything to fit their own theories of life. Others are only interested in miracles because they are greedy to tap into the power they exhibit. God doesn't often use spectacular miracles to reach people, but sometimes He knows that a special exhibition of His love and care is just what people need. When Jesus healed the eyes of the man born blind, the religious leaders were more upset than convinced of anything. They feared that this new miracle would strengthen Jesus' position with the people. But to the blind man himself, the miracle was crystal clear proof of Who Jesus was.

Have you ever seen something you would consider a miracle? How did it affect you? List some of the non-spectacular answers to prayer that you have seen recently. Thank God for His personal involvement in your life and be sure to share these small miracles with the searching and hurting people around you.

_____
_____
_____
_____
_____
_____
_____
_____
_____
_____
_____
_____
_____

DAY 7: **The Straight Scoop**

Jesus answered, "If you want to be perfect, go, sell your possessions and give to the poor, and you will have treasure in heaven. Then come follow me. When the young man heard this, he went away sad, because he had great wealth (Matthew 19:21-22).

Jesus knew how to tailor His method according to the individual He spoke with, but He never tailored the message. Sometimes we make the mistake of trying to soften the truth to make it seem more attractive. We stay away from uncomfortable things like sin, punishment, or giving up things we want, and instead present only the "good stuff." We like to talk about love, healing, personal fulfillment, and happiness. But that is not the whole story. God is not interested in commitments that are based only on "what I can get out of it," or "as long as I don't have to give up anything," or "just until it gets hard." He does not want to lure people into the His Kingdom with false promises of an easy, trouble-free life.

This young man thought of himself as righteous and God-fearing. He may have been expecting Jesus to tell him that he was already acceptable to God, and needed nothing else. But Jesus knew what was in his heart, and He showed the young man where his priorities really were misplaced. The young man wanted God, but only in second place.

Write down the essentials of the coming to faith in Jesus Christ. What is the cost? What are the rewards?

_____

_____

_____

_____

_____

_____

_____

_____

_____

_____

DAY 8: **That Guy? You've Got to Be Kidding!**

"Lord," Ananias answered, "I have heard many reports about this man and all the harm he has done to your saints in Jerusalem." ... But the Lord said to Ananias, "Go! This man is my chosen instrument to carry my name before the Gentiles and their kings and before the people of Israel" (Acts 9:13,15).

We are supposed to be prepared to tell others about Jesus Christ, but sometimes God sends us to talk to some unlikely seekers. Ananias had every reason to be astonished at God's direction, because Saul (later called Paul) had been doing his best to destroy anyone who claimed to follow Christ. He was the last man any Christ-follower of the time would have dreamed of sharing the new life in Christ with. It is easy to categorize people, but it is also easy to be wrong about the categories we put them in. We clearly need God's vision for seekers—the kind of vision that includes the unlikely, the "undesirable," the people that no one would dream of reaching out to.

Ask God to give you His vision for seekers. As you pray, what individuals or group of people is God giving you a passion for? How can you respond with action?

_____

_____

_____

_____

_____

_____

_____

_____

_____

_____

_____

DEVOTIONALS

DAY 9: **Starting From Scratch**

Paul then stood up in the meeting of the Areopagus and said: "Men of Athens! I see that in every way you are very religious. For as I walked around and looked carefully at your objects of worship, I even found an altar with this inscription: TO AN UNKNOWN GOD. Now what you worship as something unknown I am going to proclaim to you (Acts 17:22-23).

Paul knew that he was talking to a group of people in Athens who had probably never heard of the God of Israel. To stand up and say, "Jesus is the long-awaited Messiah!" would mean absolutely nothing to them. They had no past relationship with the one true God as the Jews had, and no prior knowledge of their own need for salvation or God's plan to send a Savior. Paul had to start from scratch, telling them who he was talking about when he mentioned God. He found something from their own culture and belief system to anchor his explanation in. He showed them he was not just referring to one god among many, but specifically to the one God who created the universe, and therefore owns it.

Our society today is becoming more and more like Athens, with very little knowledge of God or the Bible, and a strong emphasis on human reason. Think of two or three different angles you could use to bring up a discussion of God and Jesus, without saying, "the Bible says."

_____

_____

_____

_____

_____

_____

_____

_____

_____

_____

_____

DAY 10: **Get Ready, Get Set, Go!**

Preach the Word; be prepared in season and out of season; correct, rebuke and encourage—with great patience and careful instruction (2 Timothy 4:2).

As we look at the examples of Jesus, the disciples, and the early Christians, we can see that sharing God's message isn't done by formula. There is no one right way that will always "work," no certain set of words to memorize, or magical steps to follow. Each situation and each person needs a little different approach. It is our job to prepare ourselves to be used by God. We do this by studying the Scriptures, by talking to Him regularly, and especially by listening to Him constantly. We need to become sensitive to God's voice so that we can hear when He gives us directions. Another key besides preparation is patience—one encounter by itself won't usually change a life.

Read 1 Peter 3:15. What are some things you could do to be better prepared to give an answer for the hope that lies within you? Ask God for a heart for people and boldness to share with them.

_____

_____

_____

_____

_____

_____

_____

_____

_____

_____

_____

_____

IGNITE

Refining and Purifying Your Faith

The Power Lunch ...
Reaching Out and
Influencing People (Zacchaeus)

Luke 19:1-10, 18:7; Acts 17:26-27

Have you ever been in a restaurant and seen two well-dressed business men or women with alligator briefcases, talking about contracts and millions of dollars? If you have, then you observed a power lunch. At a power lunch, decisions are made, cash flows and sometimes the whole direction of a corporation changes.

Two thousand years ago, Jesus attended a power lunch in the city of Jericho with a man named Zacchaeus. The Bible doesn't record what Jesus said to Zacchaeus, but after this power lunch, Zacchaeus was never the same.

START IT UP

Eating lunch with Jesus must have felt like a great honor to Zacchaeus.

1. **Who is the most "important" person you have shared a meal with? (Or met personally?)**

2. **What would you do if Jesus invited you to lunch? What do you think you two might talk about?**

TALK IT UP

Today, as we discuss the story of Jesus' meeting Zacchaeus, we'll focus on three things this story can teach us about how we should live our lives.

Read Luke 19:1-10

Zacchaeus was anything but righteous—in fact, the guy was a crook—despised and hated because he was a tax collector. At that time, Rome ruled the nation of Israel and demanded heavy taxes of the people. Tax collectors not only forced people to pay these taxes, but they overcharged and kept the extra for themselves. The citizens could do nothing about it because the tax collectors were in with the Roman government. Jewish tax collectors were despised by the Romans who hired them to do their dirty work and considered traitors by their fellow Jews. A tax collector could grow rich, but he was an outcast of society.

What's the Attraction?

Zacchaeus was seeking some answers—truth about life and meaning for his existence. Zacchaeus had heard about Jesus and he "wanted to see who Jesus was." Zacchaeus knew who he was—he was a sinner, an outcast in society, and a cheat. Yet at the same time, he was a seeker. He wasn't satisfied with the way his life was working. He'd heard about Jesus, and there was something about Jesus that attracted him. Finding out about Jesus might have been scary, yes. But it caught his attention.

It's the same today. People want to see who Jesus is. Is Christianity for real? Is it authentic? It sounds sort of weird, but it sounds attractive too. Zacchaeus wanted to see Jesus, but he couldn't see because of the crowd. He was short and the people were blocking his view.

3. **What sorts of things do you think are the biggest "view-blockers" or "turn-offs" for seekers as they look at the Christians they know?**

Our Christian cliques and our stained glass fortresses may keep people out rather than welcoming them in. To really be an asset, we talk about living our lives the way Jesus did, applying God's radical truths in our lives, and sharing the good news of Jesus with other people. But does your life match your message? Here is a great test: Would you do this particular activity if Jesus were sitting across the table from you? If the answer is yes, go for it. It if is not, that could be a warning sign.

4. **What do you think you personally could do to be more inviting and welcoming to seekers?**

God ... Not Far From Each Person

Read Luke 18:17

This story of Zacchaeus is pretty amazing! Remember, Zacchaeus wasn't just any old tax collector. He was the manager of all the tax collectors in Jericho. He was a man of great wealth and yet when he heard the news of Jesus coming, he acted like a little kid. He ran and he climbed up a tree so he could see. This is a concept we should all remember. Even after we have become Christ-followers, we can become too concerned with our own importance and think we are too dignified to follow Him wholeheartedly. Zacchaeus didn't care what others thought of him. He was only concerned with Jesus.

Read Acts 17:26-27

Funny how Jesus just "happened" to walk under the exact tree Zacchaeus had chosen. When we come to Jesus, we tend to think that we have "found God." This is a bit of a joke because, in reality, God finds us. We blunder along, with a dim idea that we need Him when all the time He is at our elbow. Just as Jesus walked under the sycamore tree, God has strategically placed people in each of our lives who have given us the nudges we needed to turn to Him. As a Christ-follower, do you realize that you might be that strategic person for someone else?

5. **Who has been one of the strategic people in your life? Does this person even know the influence he or she had?**

"Seeker-Colored" Glasses

Jesus had eyes to see the hurting and seeking people around Him. He noticed Zacchaeus and so many others because people mattered to Him. Many times, we miss opportunities to introduce people to Jesus simply because we don't notice people. We need to ask God to give us His lenses. Invite God to open your eyes and you'll begin to see a "Zacchaeus" perched in his sycamore tree—or next to you in the office, the grocery store or the house next door.

It's easy, once we accept Jesus Christ, to decrease our circle of friends who don't know Christ. Sometimes we do need to get out of relationships that are incompatible with our new life in Jesus. Our closest connections need to be with people who will build us up in the faith. But we still need to have relationships with those who are still seeking. Now, we can't say, "I am building a relationship with this seeker as I go get drunk." If we are joining in their lifestyle in order to "connect," they are not going to change—we are. At the same time, we must learn to build bridges of integrity with those who don't know Christ.

6. What do "bridges of integrity" look like?

In addition, we can never look at seekers with assaulting eyes. Some people think that sharing the good new of Jesus' gospel is a contest. The more people they drag into church, the more rewards they will get. As they are inviting you to attend, you can see them covertly etching another notch in the back of their Bibles. "Ha! Got another one." If this is your attitude, people can see it a mile away. They will see and say, "This person doesn't care about me personally. I am just another notch." Sharing the good news of Jesus is about letting God's love flow through us; it's not about us at all. We have to share the good news, not thinking about ourselves or our rewards, but rather focusing on the true needs of the people around us.

7. How do you respond when you feel like someone is being friendly to you in a "fake" way? How can you avoid seeming "fake" when you reach out to others?

If we list the characteristics of Jesus, it reads something like this: love, grace, power, strength, forgiveness, the Savior, and so on. But how many of us would remember the fact that Jesus was the friend of sinners? When you read the books of Matthew, Mark, Luke, and John, you see again and again that Jesus was criticized for associating with sinners. Jesus didn't join in with their sinful lifestyles. But He loved them and He showed it. So should we. Can you call yourself a "friend of sinners? Are you the "avoider of sinners"? Or maybe you're just a "sinner."

If we live our Christian lives just soaking in the good stuff, we will become spiritually waterlogged. If you want to see joy, excitement, and thrills ... step out of your comfort zone and share some of your faith and reason for hope. Go ahead, talk to that person who is dishonest, antisocial or throwing their life down the drain. And don't just say, "Uh, will you come to church?" and then hand them over to the "experts" with a sigh of relief. Too many times people call up the pastor and say, "I found a seeker—will you come lead this person to Christ?" No way. That's your job. If you are the one God sent to walk under that person's sycamore tree, then you are the one God intends to share with him or her. Sure, you'll feel uncertain. You may not know what to say, or worry about saying the wrong thing. But remember, this thing isn't about you. God loves that seeker. God is right at your elbow and He will show you when and how to speak the words of truth. When you have the Holy Spirit on your side, even the most ordinary person can be a powerful evangelist.

Secret Agent or Change Agent?

What changes have you made, personally and publicly, as a result of you relationship with Jesus? Zacchaeus had a change of heart, and this change immediately affected his public life. Right there in front of everyone, he acknowledged that he had sinned and promised to make it right. Zacchaeus didn't just make an "intellectual assent" to the truth. He had faith with shoes on. It is the same for you today. If Jesus Christ has changed your life, then people will be able to see it. If your faith is for real, other people will be able to see love, vitality, conviction, and compassion flowing from your life. They will see your clay feet too. The flaws will show, but they should also see you humbly acknowledging these flaws. They will see Jesus in the way you act and react. If people are surprised when they eventually find out that you are a Christian, then it's time for a serious self-examination.

8. **Do you think people around you know that you are a Christian? What is it about you that would give them this message?**

LIFT IT UP

We all get so comfortable in our easy lifestyles; we don't like to be shaken up. We resist changing our behavior or our friends. But if you will let yourself be shaken a little, you might begin to notice seekers around you. As you build those relationships and live to showcase Christ, your life will come alive like never before. Real living is sometimes embarrassing or uncomfortable. But if we check out of real life because we are afraid of the hard things, we are also discarding the joy, excitement, and adventure. We will miss out on all the best parts—all that gives life zest and real purpose. God is calling us off the spiritual couch, out into the sun and wind to run with Him. Will you go?

9. **What do you feel is your biggest hang-up that is most likely to prevent you from connecting with seekers or sharing about God?**

10. **Have you ever said to God, "Whatever you want, no matter what"? If not, what is holding you back? If you have, where do you need a fresh reminder or boost?**

Identify one seeker within the each group member's circle of influence. Then take time to pray together for both the seekers and for ways you can reach out to them with the love of Jesus.

My Prayer Needs:

_____

_____

_____

_____

My Group's Prayer Needs:

_____

_____

_____

_____

_____

_____

_____

_____

_____

_____

LEADER'S GUIDE

Whether you're a brand new small-group leader or a longtime veteran, this leader's guide is designed to help you make the most of your group time. It will help you facilitate a healthy discussion among the members of your group, as well as provide you with insight and answers to questions in each session. Remember to check here not only for answers to questions you are unsure about, but also for ideas on how to involve everyone, and how to bring creativity to the discussions.

Throughout this study there are a few places where you will encounter large sections of Scripture to read. As the leader, you should encourage members of your group to come to your meeting time prepared, having read the session, checked Scripture references, and answered the questions. That way you can summarize these large blocks rather than risk losing people's attention while someone reads aloud. But, be careful not to assume everyone knows these Bible stories, and make sure your summaries give the important points. Doing this will help you maintain a smooth flow in the discussion as you stay on target (and on time) in your group.

Leading a small group can be challenging, but it also brings many rewards, so invest some time in preparing yourself to lead. You'll be delighted with the results!

Session One – What Floats Your Boat? ... Listening to God

Objectives:
- Identify the benefits of listening to God
- Discover how to listen to God as we face daily decisions

1. Have you ever had a dog or other pet? Did this pet come when you called or did it totally ignore you? Would it come for anybody else?

2. When you are in a crowded room, is there one particular sound you are more likely to notice than other sounds? Why?
   Tip: You can transition out of these start-up questions by saying, "Listening is more than just hearing; it is focusing on what is being said and responding to it. Today we're going to look at how Noah focused on God's voice and responded to what He commanded."

3. Have you ever done something that other people thought was crazy? What was your perspective on the situation? What do you think God's perspective was?
   Tip: "Crazy" in this context means something risky, not something silly (Examples: bungee jumping, taking a new job with less pay).

4. When have you pushed past a "quitting point"? How big does that wall or obstacle look to you now from this side?
   Tip: A good follow-up question could be, "What gave you the strength and endurance to push through?"

5. When has God given you a "build the boat" assignment? How did you respond to the details?

6. What types of details do you worry or wonder about as you think about trying to obey God in your current circumstances?

7. When have you seen an example of the difference between God's timing and your timing? Was it worth the wait?
   Tip: To find out more, follow up with the question, "How long was it before you recognized it was worth the wait?"

8. What do you think your first reaction would be if you were stepping on dry ground again after a year on a boat with a bunch of smelly animals?

9. How can you demonstrate an attitude of thankfulness and worship in your day-to-day life?

10. Whose voices are your ears trained to hear?
    Friends or peers, parents, co-workers, leaders, children, etc.

11. As you honestly evaluate your life, what things grab your attention and ignite your passion?
    Tip: This is to help identify the things that are most important to us.

12. What kind of training have you been giving your ears? How much time do you spend each day focused on your relationship with God?
    Tip: In other words, what do your ears hear the most? (Examples: movies, music, criticism, and opinions of others). Follow-up: How does this input impact your ability to hear God?

13. Do you think you might have some communication barriers between you and God? Ask Him to show you the sins in your life and then confess them to Him and repent.
    Tip: This question may be tough for some to open up on, but it can also help generate prayer requests.

LEADER'S GUIDE

Session Two – Great Walls of Fire ... Finding Confidence in Adversity

Objective:
- Learn how to walk with God through the "fiery" crises of life

1. Have you ever had dreams about fires? If so, what key details do you remember about them?

2. Today, how do you feel about fire? Does it fascinate or frighten you? What might have influenced your attitude toward fire?
   Tip: A transition out of these start-up questions could be, "Fire is usually seen as destructive—and it certainly is in the story we're going to study in this session—but God takes what was meant to be destructive and makes it instructive. Through this fire story, we can learn how to walk through the fire rather than being consumed by it."

3. What are some examples of real-life crises that we could identify as "fiery furnaces"? How would personal knowledge of God's character help a person deal with these things?
   We are better able to trust someone we know deeply. If we know that God is faithful, good, loving, just, gracious, and merciful, then it helps us to trust Him as we walk through the fire.

4. Where are you most tempted to compromise? Can you behave differently with different groups of people without compromising? How far can you go without being disobedient?
   Tip: Read and discuss 1 Corinthians 9:19-23, 1 Corinthians 10:23-11:1, and Galatians 1:10.

5. Why doesn't God always rescue His people from the fiery furnaces of life? Is it still worth following Him without a guarantee that He will rescue you? Why?
   Tip: Read and discuss Job 2:1-10. If our ultimate purpose is to glorify God, then that purpose is sometimes better accomplished through difficult circumstances.

6. What character qualities are produced by "fire" in our lives? Why do you think these particular qualities come out of "fiery" experiences?
   Tip: Read James 1:2-4 to understand how God uses trials in our lives.

7. When have you been in the furnace with God? What did you learn through the experience? Do you think it brought you closer to reflecting His image?

8. What is this world's definition of success? What do you think God's definition of success is? Which definition do you really live by?
   Tip: Read Joshua 1:7-10.

9. Read Daniel 3:28 again. Do you think anyone would be able to say this about you? What things in our lives might come under the category of "serving" or "worshiping" another god?
   Materialism, professional success, sex, appearance, money, etc.

10. How can this group pray for you as you are walking through the fires of life?

11. What results of previous fires can you thank God for?

Session Three – Lion Food ...
Developing Courage

Objectives:
   • Understand the different kinds of courage we need to exhibit
   • Apply courage-building steps in our lives

1. When you were growing up, what were you most afraid of?

2. Identify a real life person whose courage you particularly admire. What makes this person especially courageous to you?
   Tip: Transition into the discussion by saying, "There are different kinds of courage that we can display in our lives. During this session, we are going to look at courage and what it takes to build courage into our lives."

3. What are things God sometimes asks us to do that might seem "weird" to the people around us?
   Pray, fast, tithe, serve in church, take a job that pays less, limit media intake, etc.

4. What are some areas of your life today where you need to maintain and strengthen your ethical courage?
   Honesty with others, integrity at work, purity in social situations, give up personal time for family time or to reach out to those in need, etc.

5. How can we show relational courage in our marriages? With our children? With our parents? With our friends?
   Work through conflict instead of ignoring it, speak honestly, express love, etc.

LEADER'S GUIDE

6. How could showing relational courage actually draw people to God?
   Tip: Follow up by reading Daniel 6:20 again and asking, "Do you think someone would describe you as a "servant of the living God." Why or why not?

7. What does it mean to meditate on the Bible (Book of the Law)? What is the result of meditating on God's Word?
   Reminds us of the truth; gives us God's perspective; clears our minds of nagging concerns, re-fills our hearts; gives faith, hope, love, peace, and courage; etc.

8. God's faithfulness in the past helps us to have courage today. What reason do you have to be courageous today?
   Tip: In other words, how has God been faithful to you in the past?

9. In what area of your life do you most need to develop your courage?
   Tip: Use this question to generate prayer requests.

10. Think about your relationships. Do you have some courageous friends who build you up? Where could you look for some people like this?

Session Four – Playing With Fire ... Seizing "Defining Moments"

Objectives:
- Recognize the defining moments we face
- Learn how to make wise "defining moment" decisions

1. What is the strangest food you have chosen from a salad bar or buffet? Do you choose quickly or do you like to take your time?

2. What is a recent decision you are glad you made?
   Tip: Transition into the discussion by saying, "It is sometimes hard to make decisions, but the decisions we make—even the seemingly small ones—can have a powerful impact on our lives. In this session, we are going to look at how to make wise "defining moment" decisions.

3. What was Lot looking at when he made his decision? What was Abraham looking at? Who got the best deal and why?

4. What are modern moral equivalents to "pitching our tents toward Sodom" – decisions that can take us one step closer to temptation?
   Developing intimacy with a person of the opposite sex when we are married, spending time in settings where we are tempted to sin, spending time with people who negatively influence us, consuming media that fills our minds with ungodly thoughts, etc.

5. What defining moment decisions are you currently facing?
   Tip: These can be listed as prayer requests. If the timing feels right, pause to pray for thee decisions right now.

6. Who do you have around you who can serve on your personal board of directors? What qualities do they exhibit that make them good advisors?
   Tip: Read Proverbs 12:5,15 and Proverbs 20:19

7. Has God ever rescued you from your own folly? How did He do it?

8. Why did God tell Lot and his family not to look back? Why did Lot's wife disobey? What might "looking back" look like in our lives today?
   Looking back indicates that our hearts are still "in Sodom." This could include: dreaming of "the good old days," holding on to relationships that you need to let go of, hanging out in places that have pulled us down in the past, etc.

9. How are your communication lines with God? Do you have a consistent prayer time? Do you ask Him for His input in all your decisions?

10. If you feel that you have already made a bad decision in a defining moment, remember that it's not too late to repent and turn away from Sodom. Lot could have faced his tent the opposite direction at any time. How can this group pray for and encourage you in defining moments or struggles in your life?

Session Five – Dry as a Bone ...
Growing in Life's Deserts

Objectives:
- Acknowledge the value of lessons learned in the "desert"
- Find out how to grow through "desert times"

LEADER'S GUIDE

1. Who is one of the most interesting people you have met?

2. What is an experience you have had that you think is unique to your group?
   Tip: Have fun with this question! You may even want to have a "prize" for the most interesting answer.

3. What kinds of experiences do you think could be metaphorically described as spiritual deserts?
   Tip: For questions 3-6, encourage different people to answer each question to save time and allow everyone the opportunity to share their experiences.

4. As you look back over your life, what are some experiences that God used to prepare you for what was ahead?

5. How do you react when you face a "desert" time in your life?

6. What good have you seen come out of a "desert" experience in your life?

7. What is the area of your life that is hardest to give to God?
   Children, marriage, relationships, singleness, job, finances, past sin, etc.

8. What has God used to get your attention recently? How has God communicated with you?
   Tip: You could follow-up with the question, "How do you know when God is communicating with you?"

9. Why was God angry with Moses? Has God ever asked you to do something that you really didn't want to do? What happened?

10. What are the deserts in your life right now? What do you think God is trying to say to you now whether or not you are in a desert time?
    Tip: Use this question to compile a list of prayer requests.

11. Have you thanked God for the desert times in your life? They don't seem fun, but God is working on us to make us into His kind of people. What specific changes or outcomes can you thank Him for?

Session Six – Fish Bait ...
Following God's Lead

Objectives:
- Understand the benefits of following God's lead
- Identify areas in which we are running from God

1. What are some of your favorite games, past and present?

2. In general, do you like to organize and direct or would you rather stay in the background? Why is that?
   Tip: Transition into the discussion by saying, "Some people like to take the lead when playing games and also when living their lives, but it is important for us to recognize Who the ultimate Leader is if we are going to live the lives God has planned for us."

3. Have you ever heard a message that you were pretty sure was from God, but you really didn't like it? How can we tell if a message is from God or not?
   Anything we believe is from God must be tested against the teachings of the Bible. If it contradicts Scripture, then it is not from God. He never contradicts Himself.

4. How can we tell whether or not favorable circumstances are God's blessings?
   See if that circumstance is consistent with Scripture (Example: If you are married and the "favorable circumstance" is that you now have the money to pay for a divorce because you just aren't happy anymore, then this is not a blessing from God.)

5. What high-priced consequences to sin have you seen or experienced?

6. What keeps you from wanting to pray when you've been running from God? Are those reasons based on truth or misconceptions about God?
   Example: If you feel God is still angry with you for past sin that you have already confessed to Him, then your feelings are based on misconceptions (see John 1:9).

7. When has God given you a second chance? How did you feel when this occurred?

8. Who do you have the hardest time seeing as someone God loves? Why do you think you feel this way? What should you do about it?
   Tip: Be sure that this discussion focuses on how we should change and not on how the other person is so "unlovable."

9. Have you been running away from something God wants you to do? It's not too late to step off the ship called "Disobedience" and start for Ninevah. Share your struggle with the group so they can pray with you.

10. Is there something God wants you to do and you want to obey, but you're still scared to move ahead on? Let this group pray with you for encouragement and strength.

Session Seven – Clash of the Titans ... Embracing Strong Convictions

Objectives:
- Recognize the importance of holding to our convictions
- Learn how to live out our convictions in today's world

1. When you were a child, did you really believe in Santa Claus? Did your belief affect your behavior in November and December?

2. Who is a person (either in history or in your life) whom you have admired because of his or her strong convictions?
   Tip: Transition by saying, "Our convictions shape our conduct. In this session we are going to look at where our convictions should come from and how we can live them out."

3. Will this "politically correct" logic lead to order and peace or disorder and chaos? Why or why not?
   Tip: Some of your group members may reflect the thinking of our current culture. Be sensitive to the differing opinions of your group, but then point them to the fact that we live in a society that has law—a "code of conduct"—that helps us to live together. Ultimately, there are some things that have to be true for all of us or our world will become chaos.

4. What are some areas where people today try to waver between opposing convictions?

5. How do you respond when the Holy Spirit reminds you of rebellion in your life? How do you respond to the messengers He sends to confront you?
   Tip: A good follow-up question could be, "Who is someone you trust to give you God's perspective?"

6. How can you tell whether you are experiencing conflict because of godly convictions or just because you are being stubborn and opinionated?
   Examine your motives. Are you driven more by love or by a desire to be right?

7. What character quality do you particularly admire in the godly people you know? How can you work on developing or strengthening this quality in your own life?

8. What things could become idols in your life? Remember, an idol is simply something that takes your attention and devotion away from God.

9. What blessings have you experienced in the past through a willingness to obey God?

10. Are you ready to say, "Whatever you want, God," and stand up for His truth? What convictions are you trying to live out? What barriers are standing in your way that this group can help you pull down?
    Tip: Though there may be an opportunity to offer advice, focus on praying for each other.

Session Eight – The Power Lunch ...
Reaching Out and Influencing People

Objectives:
- Identify ways we can better reach out to those who are seeking Christ
- Examine our lives for areas that are compromising our credibility

1. Who is the most "important" person you have shared a meal with? (Or met personally?)

2. What would you do if Jesus invited you to lunch? What do you think you two might talk about?
   Tip: If you have group members who are not yet Christ-followers, then begin your discussion by explaining that this session is about how to reach out to those who want to know more about God (we are referring to them as "seekers"). Because we have all been seekers at one time in our lives, this is a great chance to honestly and humbly discuss how we can better share what God has given us.

3. What sorts of things do you think are the biggest "view-blockers" or "turn-offs" for seekers as they look at the Christians they know?
   Tip: Just brainstorm a list of ideas. Don't spend time discussing whether or not these perceptions are fair or not.

LEADER'S GUIDE

4. What do you think you personally could do to be more inviting and welcoming to seekers?
   Tip: You might lead in to this question by asking, "How did Jesus reach out to people?"

5. Who has been one of the strategic people in your life? Does this person even know the influence he or she had?

6. What do "bridges of integrity" look like?
   Be honest with them, don't compromise your convictions, spend time together without an agenda, love them instead of judging them, etc.

7. How do you respond when you feel like someone is being friendly to you in a "fake" way? How can you avoid seeming "fake" when you reach out to others?
   Make sure your actions are a result of love for others and not because of a personal agenda.

8. Do you think people around you know that you are a Christian? What is it about you that would give them this message?

9. What do you feel is your biggest hang-up that is most likely to prevent you from connecting with seekers or sharing about God?

10. Have you ever said to God, "Whatever you want, no matter what"? If not, what is holding you back? If you have, where do you need a fresh reminder or boost?

Acknowledgements

Creating a small-group study is an amazingly complex task, and it is not just one man's effort. I truly appreciate the effective partnership between Fellowship Church and Serendipity House, as well as the individuals who contributed to this resource.

Fellowship Church:
Key contributors on the editorial and design team were Andy Boyd, Tianne Moon, and J.P. Ratigan.

Serendipity House Publishing:
Key contributors on the editorial and production team were Kathy Bence, Ben Colter, Katharine Harris, and Scott Lee. Final design and typesetting were provided by Joe Moore of Powell Creative, Inc.

Great job team!